Smoke Rings
Over the Valley

Smoke Rings Over the Valley

By ROY GALLINGER

North Country Books
Utica, New York

SMOKE RINGS OVER THE VALLEY

Copyright © 1970
by
Roy Gallinger

ISBN 0-925168-74-2

First printing 1970
Fay Edward Faulkner Printing Company
Heritage Press
Sherburne, New York

First paperback printing 2001

NORTH COUNTRY BOOKS
311 Turner Street
Utica, New York 13501

Dedicated to
Our Young Friends
DAVE AND SANDRA WOLFANGER
Whose married lives remind us of
our early wedded years.

PROLOGUE

History is like a dream — a dream gone past. It was once alive, vibrant and throbbing with reality. Today it is still alive in memory and memory never dies. It is that second life without which mankind would never be complete.

The stories told in this book once lived. The characters once moved, and were once a big part of the life in Chenango County. They lived and were loved by people of yesterday and without them there might never have been a people to build our forests into cities and our valleys into homes and farms.

It may seem only yesterday when these fertile lands were hills and forests. It seems only yesterday when pure streams of sparkling water coursed over these lands, bringing refreshment and nourishment to those to whom God had directed to live in this beautiful country. This valley He has set like a green jewel among the hills and along the placid river the Indians named "Chenango."

It often takes a white hot crucible to bring out the gold from the dross. By the same token it takes both rain and sunshine, snow and cold, war and famine to bring out a final joy and peace. So it is with history. There must be bloodshed in the forest and death on the battlefield in order that a kindly peace may spread like a benediction over the land.

The crashing thunderbolts of the past have finally cleared the air allowing the raindrops of hope to give place to peace and prosperity.

The stories in this book have been gathered by the author over a period of years and are as authentic as research and records allow.

Roy Gallinger

TABLE OF CONTENTS

9

THE FATE OF WALTER GERMAN

The mystery surrounding the final days of the first settler in North Norwich, in Chenango County, reads like a paper-back novel.

The lives of his family and the consequences that led to the depredation of a well known and industrious name, should live in Chenango history.

General Obadiah German died penniless and under mysterious circumstances, his money wrenched from him by a brother-in-law, leaving an ominous impression of crime. No one knows what happened to the general's $60,000, which was a lot of money in those early days of the last century.

General Obadiah German came to North Norwich in 1796 to take over his grant of land, earned by his involvement in the Revolutionary War. He opened a log store, the first trading post in the area at the intersection of what is now Route 12 and the East River Road. He was happy with his wife and two sons and two daughters. He prospered. The General was thrifty and made purchases of land as soon as he obtained sufficient funds. He became a great land owner and in fact owned what is now the entire township of German, in the southwest corner of the county. A leader, he was soon elected to public office and became assemblyman, and later was the first Chenango County Judge.

General German prospered and when politics took him away from home, he set up his youngest son, Walter, in the retail business, in the center of the present North Norwich village.

Walter was a young man of talent and when his father became a member of the assembly, he also took over the Trading Post. He proved to be an astute business man and honest to a fault. As he prospered, he built a more modern store. It was the first store with large display windows in the county and contained a stock of goods from sugar and tobacco to coal oil, buffalo robes, calico and plows. Rigs came from miles around to trade with the kindly proprietor.

11

At the height of the industrious young man's career, whispers of another war threatened. Walter organized a company of militia and daily practices were held on the green across from his store. When the War of 1812 was declared, the young merchant enlisted his company. Little did he know when he signed his name with the quill pen that he would never return.

Amid tears from wives, mothers and sweethearts, the men, headed by a single fife, marched out of sight.

Walter German had placed the business in his brother Albert's keeping and the business continued to prosper. The profits were faithfully kept against the day when Walter would return.

One day a courier galloped into the hamlet with news that Walter was dead. The messenger had a story but no one was to hear it, except Albert, and even he did not hear the whole truth. The courier and Albert went to the back of the store, for privacy, and after the courier had left, and Albert recovered from the shock, it was learned that Walter had died in a hangman's noose for a serious infraction of army rules. No one ever learned just what the infraction was.

When the people heard the news they were stunned. What wrong could he have done to deserve such an ignominious death? He was known for his honesty and regard for his fellow man. To have him die at the end of a rope, after a court martial, did not seem possible.

The death of their favorite son devastated the whole community. His mother never recovered and a few days later died, still whispering his name. The name of the boy who at that moment was lying in a dishonorable grave.

Albert, discouraged, sold the business and as if Fate had taken a hand, the new owner was nearly bankrupt when he sold it to another. This owner failed after only a few months and the store was closed and stood vacant for two years. Then another man tried to make a go of it but spent all his wealth trying to profit.

Finally the town bought the property and turned it into a schoolhouse. Later it was used for a church, then a grange hall and town hall and even the post office was situated there for a while. It seemed that nothing could prosper there again. Some old timers say that it was an indication that the death of Walter German was a miscarriage of justice. In 1967 the building was demolished, perhaps the oldest standing wooden structure in the county at that time.

After the death of his wife and son, the General, wealthy for his time, chose to suffer out his grief alone. This made him a prime target for a designing young woman who came his way in the form of a shapely beauty. No one seemed to know just where she came from, but the lively lady made herself so interesting to the old man that he asked her to become his wife.

This information comes from a letter written during the Civil War signed by his daughter, Mrs. Harmon, who lived in Camillus, at that time.

It seems the young lady accepted before the General could change his mind and they were married. Shortly thereafter the new wife sent for her brother, a slick schemer, from the East. Together they planned to get hold of the General's money.

The brother managed to get the old gentleman's signature on a series of notes, which he immediately cashed and then left town. The General became penniless.

Mrs. Harmon further states that her father then died under mysterious circumstances. He was alone with his wife and a servant. At that time there were no autopsies nor ways to determine the exact cause of death. According to the letter, the General died of an overdose of some narcotic. The neighbors were too trusting to pin anything on the vivacious young widow.

After the funeral, the young lady left on the stage to Syracuse and from there to a western state, where she met her brother.

But retribution lay ahead, Mrs. Harmon's letter says.

When the beautiful young lady demanded her share, her brother refused and a quarrel ensued. Then he literally bounced

13

her out on her ear, and she never received a cent of her husband's estate.

In desperation, still shapely and vivacious she sought to earn a living in devious ways. She traveled the country, trying to get by on her husband's reputation as a statesman and for a time was successful.

A few years of this kind of living and her looks began to fade and her health failed. Men grew tired of her and just before the Civil War she died a broken but unrepentant woman.

ADRIFT IN A WASHTUB

Hatch Lake, in Madison County, just north of Chenango County, lies in vernal tranquility, as the waters of early spring roll against its pebbled shores. The hills that surround this sparkling lake are high enough to be picturesque, but still rolling enough to give the appearance of great distance.

To those who like stories of yesterday the tiny whitecaps on the jewel-like lake hold a tale of suspense, one that a parent of today would never like to endure. Yet it actually happened to a young pioneer over a hundred years ago.

Jane and Oliver Wescott came to the shores of Hatch Lake about 1840, and built their home. Oliver worked by the day for the early farmers of the wild community and at other times apprenticed himself to a tanner with the hopes of learning that trade. His work kept him away from home all day and from his wife and two children, ages four and six.

Jane Wescott sang as she worked in the rude cabin on the lake shore, and daily the children amused themselves by tossing pebbles into the lake or picking berries near the cabin. Jane was happy even though she was hundreds of miles away from her home and relatives in the East. There were no neighbors as yet, but she and Ollie were determined to carve out a life in the wilderness for themselves and their family.

One spring day, in April, Jane Wescott had finished the washing and had turned the wooden washtub upside down on the shore to dry and proceded to go inside the cabin to do some baking.

Elizabeth, just turned four, and her big brother, nearly six, were prattling away outside and then suddenly Jane realized it was very quiet. She thought the children might have wandered away into the woods and rushed outside.

The distracted mother looked out onto the glassy water. A modern mother would have fainted! There, almost in the center of the lake, was her washtub, with two little heads upright above its rim. A spring wind had come up and the little tub was bobbing along on the waves.

Jane's children were on the lake, which was probably 40 feet deep at that point, and the washtub could easily capsize if one of the children attempted to stand up.

Gusts of wind blew them further and further away from the cabin site. Jane didn't dare call to them for fear they would get excited and tip over. She breathed a hasty, but fervent prayer and started around the shore to the other side of the lake. Tearing her legs on the briars and with sobs choking her, she finally got around to the spot to which it seemed the tub was heading.

The wind seemed to slow to a gentle breeze and the tub stopped revolving and kept drifting toward her, where she hid in the bushes. No one knows how many times she thanked God that the lake had calmed.

As the improvised craft scraped on the shore the distraught mother ran out from the bushes, her knees weak from the strain. Splashing into the water she grasped both children in her arms and as she splashed out onto the dry pebbles with her precious armful, she dropped to her knees in prayer and then fainted.

In a few minutes she recovered and with her children made her way back to the cabin.

Hatch Lake still shimmers in the April sunshine. The old timers and Indians who have heard the legend still say that it was the Great Spirit that saved Jane Wescott and her children that bright day so long ago. Some go as far as to say that because of that, the lake is usually calm in April, as the gentle whitecaps creep across the blue water and disappear on the other side where a washtub safely deposited its precious cargo.

The story of Jane Wescott has become a legend in that part of Madison County and is still told and retold around the firesides of that community.

THE DEDICATION OF MAN TO MAN

The tiny village of Plymouth, nestled in the hills a few miles northwest of Norwich, has hidden away in the yellowing pages of its history, a heart-warming story of sacrifice, bordering on the heroic.

It is a story of three country doctors who gave their lives for the people of the community who were sick — people who were dying at the rate of two or three a day, until the weary community was becoming decimated.

It was early in the last century and Plymouth was a struggling settlement. There was a general store, a church, a few homes, and the home and office of Dr. Jesse Grant. Dr. Grant, working alone in a large territory, was so busy that he sat up late at night compounding his own pills and medicine. As Dr. Grant aged, a new doctor came to work with him, a young Dr. Cyrus French, little knowing that his first charge was also to be his last, and that he would be called upon to make the supreme sacrifice in his profession.

One morning Dr. French was called to a home in the snow-bound hills. A young girl had been stricken with a fever. The young doctor ministered to the patient, but was puzzled. He came back and talked the matter over with Dr. Grant and the two men visited the patient. The malady, now long forgotten, was one for which there was no remedy at that time, and one that was particularly contagious and usually fatal.

The next day there were three more cases, and within days the entire community was in a state of confusion as more and more persons contacted the illness. Then the patients began to die.

The two doctors worked day and night, traveling the roads to bring as much relief as possible to the delirious patients, and to soothe the feelings of others in the family, preparing them for the angel of death, as their's was the work of both physician and clergyman.

17

Battling against great odds the two men fought on. Dr. Grant was the first to fall by the wayside, as his aging strength waned. He was taken to live with friends at Greene, where he later died, possibly the first victim among the heroic doctors of that day.

Young Dr. French struggled on alone, showing more each day the effect of the work he was doing. He went without food and sleep to minister to the sick, who were still dying every day. The work was telling on his resistance, and many days he could hardly put the harness on his faithful horse.

It has been said that "God tempers the wind to the shorn lamb," and one day another young doctor, Dr. Edmund Bancroft, drove into the village to be of assistance to the tired Dr. French. Together the men battled both the uncontrollable disease and the elements. By the time spring came there was scarcely a house in the community where one or more graves had not been dug through the frozen crust as the last resting place of loved ones. Literally hundreds had died during that terrible winter.

By the time the first robin came in that fateful year of 1811, both doctors were fatigued beyond recovery. Dr. Bancroft lingered for nearly a year, and then succumbed to the very disease which had taken so many of his patients. He is buried somewhere in the town of Plymouth.

Dr. French, also broken in body and spirit, was unable to carry on and gave up his practice to a younger man and moved to the hills of Pharsalia, hoping to regain his health. After two years, he, too, was laid low with the same disease and today lies buried in an unknown grave among the Pharsalia hills.

The names of Dr. Cyrus French, Dr. Jesse Grant and Dr. Bancroft are never mentioned now, but the works of these heroic men should live on, as do the names of other local heroes, in the hearts of those who came after.

This is not a big story, but it is one of those heart warming sagas that makes this county so interesting. It is a story of man's love for man and of the superhuman strength of which man is capable if the need comes.

From these men, the early doctors of pioneer days, much was gained to add to medical science. The knowledge of such a humble beginning made many strides toward the fast efficient medicine now available.

PRESTON

In 1840 the town of Preston was a thriving four-corners village, high in the hills of Chenango County. Approximately 60 families were nestled in its confines, each owning their own piece of land and being very self-sufficient.

Preston center boasted a green, set aside as a park in the center of town. Remnants of this park can still be seen although the roads have nearly pushed it out of existance. Here the boys played handball or just horsed around in the summertime. Fox and Geese was a favorite pastime on the park after a new fallen snow, but children of that day did not have so much time to spend on recreation as they do now.

The park and roads were kept up by an agreement among the settlers that each man over 21 was assessed so many days a year for road work, at least one day a year or he paid a fine of one dollar to the village clerk! There were no taxes, and for the amount of traveling done, this arrangement was sufficient. As one old timer said, "Nobody was in such a hell of a hurry in those days."

Each family owned 2 or 3 cows, a horse or oxen for heavy hauling, a pig or two, a flock of chickens and perhaps a few ducks and geese.

Barns were small one story affairs about 30 by 40 feet with lean-tos on one side where the cows were stabled in the winter. Hay was kept in the barn and during the summer the cows were milked in the yard and kept in the pasture. In October or November the cows were bred. In the spring a new calf arrived and milking was resumed.

During the summer the farmers made butter from the cream and kept it in firkins. In the fall they would sell the butter and settle up any debts. Most farms had a hired man six months of the year, and he was paid with the butter money. Every farmer raised his own meat, grain, vegetables, and some places had an orchard. The wild berries and nuts were widely used in jams and jellies. The fall was a busy season, with the butchering to be done, depended on corning, pickling, smoking

20

or outdoor freezing for preservation. Potato digging, cabbage cutting and storing, drying the corn, apples and herbs took much time and work by the family.

A few years later it was thought that a cheese factory in Preston would be an asset to the farm families and they built it just across the bridge going west from the center. This took the milk off the farm. The farmers received whey in part payment for their milk, which was fed to the calves and pigs. Then came the enterprising Rushmore and Borden. They explained the profit to be gained by producing winter milk. This meant feeding grain and building larger barns.

A man by the name of Emery Lewis is credited with building the first barn in which to milk cows during the winter. According to one old timer, when the businessman started telling the Preston farmer how to run his farm, this started the farmer's demise. And when the automobile came, it finished him off.

Around 1840 Preston could boast of many industries.

On the road south from the corners towards Oxford was the largest tannery in central New York. It was run by Samuel Hall. The main building was two stories high and about 50 feet wide and 60 feet long. On the 2nd floor hemlock bark was stored, dried and ground in a grinding machine powered by a water wheel, which was on the outside of the building. As the bark was ground it went down a chute into a bin on the first floor. A boy of 10 or 12 could earn 18 cents a day running this machine. A 12 hour day, too!

Outside, covering an eighth of an acre were vats made of 2 inch planks, 5 feet deep and 3 feet wide and 6 feet long. In the summer these vats were filled with hides in a solution of water and ground bark. Every day the hides were removed onto a platform and more bark added. This was to tan the hides evenly.

Adjoining the tannery was a currier shop where the hides were finished. The large ones were used for harness leather and the small ones for shoes and boots.

Next door was a shoe shop, where 3 or 4 men worked the year around. A customer needing new boots, which sold for around 63 cents a pair, was measured by the clerk and

21

could see his boots cut out, right then. The pieces of leather were put together and finished by the other workers. Sometimes it took a few days before the new boots were ready.

Between the center and the tannery on the left side of the road was a distillery. Here whiskey was made from potatoes. After a family reserved its winter supply of potatoes, any left over was sold to the distillery. Any farmer "worth his salt" would buy a barrel of whiskey in the fall. It was good medicine for man and beast, a well-known remedy for everything from snake bite to chill blains and in between.

Just to the east of Preston there was a sawmill and a large dam. In the spring a huge pile of logs surrounded the mill. The water from the mill pond furnished the water for the tannery and distillery also.

The saw mill was owned by a batchelor, Abel Childs, who took turns boarding with different families in the village.

Around this time Preston contained two blacksmith shops, a cheese-box factory, grindstone quarries, a three-story hotel and two churches.

The hotel was run by Judge John Noyes. The stage from Norwich stopped there on its way to Pitcher. Always a number of residents came to greet the stage. One of these was an elderly gentleman, Judge Falk. No one knows why he was called Judge, except he read his Bible every day. He was a handyman around town and had a philosophy of his own. When one would ask him how his wife was, he would say, "I'm afraid she's a little better." He declared he could prove there were no women in Heaven, because the Bible says at one time silence reigned in Heaven for the space of 5 minutes.

The school was located right at the corners and many of its scholars went on to higher fields after receiving their 3 R's in Preston. Legrand Powers graduated from Preston and became a professor in a Washington college.

Another Preston boy, Gager Throop, married a local girl and moved to Chicago, in 1839. At that time Chicago was a small village and he knew every man who lived there. He made a fortune and went to Pasadena, Calif. for the winter. They liked it so well they made it their permanent home. Mr. Throop proceeded to build a Universalist church and hired his own minister. He also established a college where a man could learn to be a minister or a blacksmith. When he died in 1899, he had the largest funeral any man had ever had up to that time in California. Just outside of Pasadena on a mountain side in huge letters is printed, "FATHER THROOP" in his memory.

When the Civil war was started the boys of Preston were anxious and many enlisted. Most of them were in the 114th regiment. Some never returned. A boy named Jay M. Scott, large for his age and eager to do his duty enlisted. He got as far as Washington, D. C. before it was discovered he was under the 14-year-old limit. His father had to go after him and bring him home.

Early in the 1800s the villagers decided they should have a public cemetery. A subscription was started and a house-to-house canvass was made for money to buy land. Everyone contributed, except one man, who flatly refused. When asked what his objections were, he stated that the piece of land they had in mind was so poor they would have to manure it before the dead could rise.

Today Preston is smaller than it ever was, with a church, fire department, a country store and a number of excellent homes. It is not too far to commute to Norwich and makes a good place to build out of the city. The high altitude is beneficial but the many farms and businesses have been swallowed by progress and state owned land.

It is still one of the prettiest little hamlets in Chenango County.

PLASTERVILLE — GHOST TOWN

There is something about a ghost town that is impressive. When one stands overlooking the spot where once homes stood, where once folks lived in peace and plenty and where once stood schools and churches, he remembers that time is a fickle dame whose caprices are unpredictable.

Such a ghost town stands about two miles north of Norwich and one today can hardly visualize in the vacant area, 200 people and two score of houses, a thriving plaster mill, to say nothing of a store, post office, tavern and the meeting house. Yet at one time the hamlet of Plasterville was an important stop on the Chenango Canal and a grand hangout for farmers on rainy days and in the winter.

Plasterville came into being just after the beginning of the 18th century and before the canal was built. The mill was built by Theodore Miller, Sr. an enterprising man and a shrewd planner.

In 1837, when the canal was built, Miller secured water rights from the canal feeder to run his mill and a large dam was constructed by the state a short distance upstream to supply water to the canal. The canal lock was built directly in front of Miller's mill, giving him about seven feet of water to gush through his mill flume, enough to turn several mills. Later when the canal was abandoned as a non-paying proposition, Miller was given the dam.

Plasterville grew when the canal came through. Timber from the Whaupaunaucau hills was hauled down to Plasterville to be sawed in a flourishing sawmill. In those days before the circular saw was invented, a crude up-and-down saw was used, a slow and laborious process, and even though lumber was plentiful, the work of processing it made it scarce.

The timbers of St. Paul's Church on Pleasant Street, in Norwich, including the huge oak beams 40 feet long, were cut in the forests of Whaupaunaucau and sawed in the mill at Plasterville.

24

In those days there were transcient mill hands, rough and ready fellows who traveled around the country but never settled down. For these hands a number of non-descript houses were built, nothing more than shacks. This part of the hamlet soon was dubbed with the unsavory name of "Pig Pen Alley." A large eel rack was installed in the flume and kept the community well supplied with fresh eels.

Limestone rock to be processed into plaster was hauled from the north, first by teams and later on the canal. The plaster was then mixed with buffalo hair, which acted as a binder and much of this early plaster is still clinging to the walls of many homes today. Wood fiber plaster has replaced the old hair plaster of yesterday.

Building materials made at Plasterville were shipped all over the state, first on the canal and later on the DL&W, a railroad that came through, sounding the death knell of the canal.

Soon after 1840 there was a great demand for sawed lumber, as the early settlers were just emerging from the log cabin period and it became fashionable and desirable to build frame houses. Some of these early frame houses, with their hand hewed corner posts, are still standing.

The main road through Plasterville was what is now known as Rt. 32 or East River Road, a secondary route parallel to Rt. 12, that passes through the city of Norwich. A stretch of land on the west side of the Chenango River, just north of Meade's Pond is still called Plasterville.

About the only building still standing is a farmhouse known for many years as the Cyrus Case house. This house was, in the heyday of Plasterville, a most important point as it housed the tavern, a store and the post office. Here came the inhabitants for their mail, their groceries and tobacco and to hear the latest canal gossip. Here the canal travelers regaled the simple villagers with stories of adventure and here the pack peddler put up for the night.

Today Plasterville is gone. The old mill burned down and another was built, but this too, is gone. Nothing remains but the old ruins of a mill wheel, the flume and the parts of a bridge. The shanties on Pig Pen Alley have disappeared, the better frame houses are gone with them. Even the eels have forsaken the river. The silent ravages of time have removed everything, from the ribald canal driver to the meeting house where the devout worshipped.

One wonders how many places in the world today, though modern and seemingly permanent, will be the ghost towns of tomorrow.

SIXTY FEET OF DAUGHTERS

The story of Capt. Daniel Brown and his 60 feet of daughters is a bright page in the history of Madison County, amid other pages of pathos, frustration and heartache, such as were endured by most of the early settlers of Central New York. These pioneers early learned to endure the hardships of frontier life, and when a bright spot appeared they were quick to grasp and make the most of it.

Capt. Brown came from Stonington, Conn., in 1791, starting out with an ox team and 14 children when he was 66. His destination was the Genesee Valley, but traveling with a plodding pair of oxen and managing 14 offspring began to tell on him.

To add to his troubles he had gotten off the path near Utica and found himself in the valley of the Unadilla, near what is now Edmeston.

The tired family stopped near the historic Percifer Carr home. Carr had settled on the east bank of the Unadilla some time before and when the Brown family came plodding along the road, Mr. Carr invited them to stop and rest. This, the wayfarers were only too glad to do.

Capt. Brown had 10 daughters, each a striking beauty and each over 6 feet tall. These were the Captain's "60 feet of daughters." Each was able to swing an ax or scythe with any man in the outfit. The daughters were named Abigail, Desire, Eunice, Lucy, Susan, Temperance, Anna, Fanny, Thede and Catherine.

As the aging Capt. Brown and Percifer Carr sat on the east bank of the river a few days after the family arrived, the old captain was taken with the beauty of that land on the other side. Carr urged him to buy and settle there and to forget the Genesee Valley. Tired as he was, the old Captain was easily persuaded.

On July 3, 1792, the captain and his four sons crossed the river. The Revolutionary War was still fresh in the mind of

27

the old soldier who had fought in that war, and he knew that back in the East, the colonies were getting ready to celebrate Independence Day. He knew that on the morrow at daybreak the cannon would roar up and down the coast.

The captain ordered his sons to grind their axes to a gleaming sharpness, before they turned in for the night. The patriotic old captain had a plan of his own.

At daybreak all hands were up. The captain stationed each at the foot of a tree and ordered them to wait for his signal. Soon he was ready. Throwing his hat into the air, the old man let out a great yell.

"God bless our country!" he cried. "Let us hew down these trees for our new civilization. This is our celebration. Go!"

Through the forest sounded the joyous yells of the boys as the trees began to fall. By nightfall a cabin awaited the captain's wife and "60 feet of daughters."

Desire was the captain's most beautiful 6 foot daughter, but she had moods of loneliness when she yearned for the East and on these occasions wanted to be by herself. She took walks into the forest, where birds and flowers seemed to soothe her nerves.

One summer day, Desire strolled into the woods and sat on a stump. In the quiet coolness, she began to sing, and noticed that an echo answered. She was intrigued and began to call into the stillness, only to hear the call echo. Once she called a long, "H-e-l-l-o!" It tickled her to hear the long drawn out echo. She tried it again and was startled by an answering, "Hello, where are you?"

Desire kept calling and the voice, now plainly masculine, kept answering. Finally through the trees came a young man, a surveyor, who had been lost in the thick forest until he heard her voice ringing over the valley. The surveyor, John I. Morgan, had turned around thinking he was heading towards Pennsylvania.

The two became fast friends. Soon Morgan returned to the East and told about the tall beautiful girl he had met in the forests of the "West." Then he started back, hoping to marry Desire, but on the way the fickle surveyor fell in love with another girl and married her, instead.

The tall beautiful Desire remained a spinster. With her sister, Temperance, she finally went to Bridgewater, where she died at the age of 91. The rest of the children married among the new settlers and remained in the community.

Thus was settled the west bank of the Unadilla, and those who suffered and those who laughed at the simple joys of the pioneer, now sleep on the hillside beside the ever flowing stream.

A BELOVED LITTLE CITY

Over a hundred years ago the last "coal oil" lamp was taken from the streets of Norwich, and its place taken by a new-fangled gas light.

Today, the streets of the city blaze with large mercury lights making it one of the best lighted of the smaller cities in the state. With the coming of two new arterial highways through the city, the bright lighted thoroughfares seem a far cry indeed from the nights of the fickering oil lamps installed on short wooden posts in the main part of what was then a "village."

As in the case of most "modern" ideas, the gaslight plan in Norwich met with strenuous opposition. A hundred reasons turned up in the minds of the citizens to be used against the plan. What if the light were blown out by the wind. The whole village would suffocate! The gas lights were too bright. Folks would go blind in a few years. And the cost — it was nothing short of sinful to use good coal in the manufacture of gas when so many people were without proper warmth in the winter. These and many other conjured-up ideas harrassed the village fathers in their attempt to modernize Norwich.

It was in 1861 and a Civil War was being fought. Against the opposition of the older residents of the village, who carried lanterns when they went downtown at night, the village board decided to allow a Syracuse man, Nathan Randall, to form a company to make gas for the town.

The younger element of the village wanted it. They had seen it in Utica and Binghamton. Others who were "ag'in" it stayed "ag'in" it but finally the "fers" won out and the contract was signed, and huge furnaces were erected in a building on Birdsall St., where the present gas plant still stands.

Then the work started in the streets as the six-inch mains were laid. Workmen digging the ditches were heckled, plagued and threatened, many workers came to the job in the morning

30

to find parts of the ditches filled in and had to shovel it all out again. The contractor had a contract to have a certain number of lights installed within a given period and he meant to keep his word. In some manner the gas works had been acquired by two wealthy Norwich men, George Ryder and Edward Hayes, and a price of $5 per 1,000 cubic feet was charged. Some die-hard customers were later given a special rate of $3 per 1,000 cubic feet as a trial offer, and there is no record of any of these going back to "coal oil" for their lighting purposes.

By degrees the oil lamps were taken away and gas put in their place. The people began to like the white lights given off by the gas jets, and more and more people had their homes piped for gas. At first those brave folks had to over-come the fear of accidential suffocation. Soon all the new homes were piped during construction, just as a building today includes wiring for electricity. Many of the older buildings in the city today still have the gas pipes in every room. A few years ago natural gas was piped into the city and is present in many modern homes and industries.

Customs change, and today the city streets blaze with a light unthought of a century ago, and future years will bring even better light. The flickering, murky light of the oil lamp on the corner is almost beyond the imagination of people today. Not even a specimen of those old lights is in existence, despite the search of historians and relic lovers.

Norwich is often called an overgrown country town. Indeed, it has been just that ever since it took on the designation of "city", an honor received while it was still under the required 10,000 population.

At one time there were more blacksmith shops than churches, and the oyster suppers served by the firemen brought out rich and poor alike. It was a town where the familiar "lunch wagon" was hauled down to the busy corner each night at dusk to provide lunches for the men about town and the late theater crowd.

Far from the beaten path, Norwich made its own fun. Circuses came in the summer, firemen held conventions and field days, the county fair became a tradition, weekly concerts played in the park during the summer, and Halloween parades were instituted in 1944, by Norwich's progressive Chamber of Commerce.

Yes, customs change — from the first pick in the hands of some unknown workman, driven in the dirt on Birdsall St. to a new era in street lighting, little knowing that in a few years even that "modern" trend would soon be antiquated.

Today, with two large shopping centers just outside of each end of the city, well lighted streets, a modern police and fire department, a radio station, a daily newspaper, a world renown pharmacal company, knitting company and foundry, it is still an overgrown country town where folks still call one another by their first names and some of the merchants still "put it on a slip" when Mrs. Jones sends her little boy in for a cake of soap or a pound of sugar.

THE WAGNERS — ARTISTS

One of the prettiest stories to come out of Chenango County since it was settled, back before 1800, is one of the least known, and it concerns a brother and sister, two of the most famous artists in the county's history. Indeed, the names of Daniel and Maria Louise Wagner, whose miniatures have become collector's items, were famous among those of high estate a century ago.

The story of the Wagners is one of "Darby and Joan" warmth and is of a brother stricken with a hip disease, who learned to draw while confined to his bed and a small sister, who inspired him to become great.

Frederick Wagner, father of the couple, was the son of a Hessian soldier. He came to Preston from Worcester, Mass. in 1806 with his wife, Annie Walworth Wagner, and a four year old son, Daniel.

Life was lonesome back in that time, but the child grew as other pioneer boys grew. At the age of 17 he was stricken with what was known in those days as hip disease, an incurable ailment.

Away from any medical help the boy lay in bed for many months. Life became dull and more dull, until one day a baby sister was born in the home and this brought a ray of light to the sick lad. The little girl became the boy's companion and once more laughter came to the one apparently doomed to a life in bed.

One day the little toddling sister brought a piece of charcoal and a bit of paper to her brother. On it he drew a rude sketch of a cow. The little girl was delighted and brought more paper and charcoal. Then, as his work improved, it dawned upon the boy that he had a talent and perhaps his life might not be wasted after all. He set to in earnest and by the time the little girl was eight, she, too, discovered a talent for art.

Together they studied as best they could with the limited means at hand in that early day. Bit by bit they picked up ideas and were soon doing silhouettes in water color. By the time Maria was 16 she was equal to her gifted brother. Now they thought they could begin to live. Daniel, through his love for his work, had overcome his hip trouble to a large degree.

The brother and sister acquired a team and a covered wagon and started to travel the countryside from Binghamton to Utica, and from Ithaca to Auburn, painting portraits and miniatures. One day they met William H. Seward of Auburn, later the governor of New York State. He was also the one who made it possible for the United States to purchase Alaska. He was so taken with the work of the two young people that he called them into his study. There he advised them to go to Albany, where he was sure they could get contracts that would pay them well.

Armed with letters of introduction from Mr. Seward, Daniel and Maria Louise set out for Albany, there to win acclaim among the elite.

They painted portraits of Martin VanBuren, Erastus Corning, Silas Wright, Millard Fillmore and many others. Great artists proclaimed the two the world's greatest painters of miniatures.

In 1852, upon the advice of Mr. Fillmore, they went to Washington. There they made paintings of Daniel Webster, President Fillmore's family and a great many other notables. Then they went to New York, where they opened a studio, and painted with oils, and where Maria Louise took up landscape painting. To her delight she found that she could do even better work with landscapes, so gave up portrait work leaving it to her brother.

Along about 1870 Daniel and Maria Wagner, still inseparable, yearned for the green hills and cool rivers of Chenango County. By that time they were situated well financially and could enjoy the remainder of their lives, painting when they wished or going on walks when the mood struck them.

They returned home and for a time taught art to a select group of students.

On February 2, 1888, Daniel Wagner died. Maria Louise would not be comforted, and on October 14th of that same year she passed on peacefully, and those who were with her at the time, say that a smile of greeting flashed across her face as the end came. Brother and sister were together again.

The miniatures done by this gifted pair are priceless today and according to some authorities there are many in existence.

In Norwich several of the older homes still possess portraits done by the boy and girl when they were traveling 'door to door in their early days.

Today they sleep side by side in the local cemetery, a long life of good deeds behind them which could not even be imagined at the time the sick boy lay on his bed on the farm at Preston.

BETTSBURG

If someone asked you the way to Bettsburg, what would you say? Most people in the vicinity of Norwich will say, "I never heard of it."

Bettsburg is on some maps, but unless the searcher knew the country in the vicinity of Afton, he might easily travel past the once thriving little hamlet without knowing it.

Bettsburg, as a village, is now little more than a ghost town. Where once the sound of the milk cans rattled in the early morning at the cheese factory, now it is still, save for the sound of speeding cars and trucks as they round the curve through what was once the heart of Bettsburg.

Bettsburg was a busy place up to about 40 years ago when the horse and buggy became extinct. As with most places, when transportation became easier, industry moved to the larger villages.

Bettsburg was born because of a land trade. In May, 1786, Elnathan Bush came from Sheffield, Mass., with his wife and four children. Bush first went to Cooperstown on horseback, and then down the Susquehanna by boat and raft, stopping at what is now known as Stowel's Island. The island, about two miles below Afton, had been cleared by that time by another settler and some Indians. The settler learned the land did not belong to him and had to move on. The island made a good stopping place for river travelers and Bush thought it would make a fine place for a home.

But the Bush family apparently did not like the island, so they loaded their worldly goods back on the raft and made their way to a tract of land in Bainbridge. They saw what they wanted, but it was owned by Hezekiah Stowel. After some negotiating, Stowel finally relented and through some unknown trade the Bush family acquired the land. There they rolled up their cabin on the site of Bettsburg, quite a way from the river.

Bettsburg, then the only settlement of any size in the southern part of the county, began to grow. A man named

36

Betts opened the first store and named the town after himself. He was succeeded by a Nathan Boynton, who was not only a doctor but owned a busy saw and grist mill at the same time.

Asa Stowel, a son of Hezekiah Stowel, also had a grist mill and a saw mill, thus the little hamlet grew. The first post office in the southern end of the country was at Bettsburg and Peter Betts was the first postmaster.

For over 100 years Bettsburg was a busy place. There was a blacksmith shop there for nearly a century and some of the finest cheese in the state came from within its borders. The cheese factory, from which came 550 pounds a day, lost business when the cheese industry became centered in larger factories and the old Bettsburg cheese factory became a dwelling.

One by one the stores and shops closed. One by one the families grew up and moved away, until today the once busy street that went through Bettsburg is marked by one fine residence that speaks of other days.

THE LEGEND OF ELLEN MacDONALD

Was it bitterness in the heart of a once-beautiful woman, stricken in the prime of her life that would cause her to turn against the world? Or was it an unquenchable woe, born of seeing a bent and twisted body, where once was beauty and symmetry?

Whatever may have been the reason, the lavish home of Ellen Douglas MacDonald in Oxford was closed and locked for 35 years.

Ellen was the daughter of Dr. George Douglas of Oxford. At one time he was a prominent and prosperous medical doctor.

From the time of early childhood the fires of joy and love burned within her. She made the most out of life and where Ellen was, there also was gaiety and laughter. She was beautiful, much sought after, and never felt the pang of need.

Indeed, life for this small town girl was the kind one reads about or which exists in the dreams of girls who are not so fortunate. She was a child of fortune.

In 1899 when Ellen was 35 and married, returning from a visit with friends in New York, the train she was riding was wrecked. She was seriously hurt and spent months in a hospital in Paterson, New Jersey. From that point in her life everything changed. Her trim and beautiful body was bent and twisted and with these changes came a bent and twisted outlook on life.

In due time her father died, then her husband, and by 1912 the little crippled lady became a little old lonely woman. Life had dealt her a body blow.

Alone in the mansion-like house on Washington Square in Oxford, her days were long and dreary. No one knows what went on in the woman's mind as she limped around the 15 rooms of the big house. Many memories must have haunted her from the past, when life was more joyful.

One day something snapped. She got up from an unfinished breakfast, put on her coat and bonnet, stepped outside and turned the key in the door, locking the ghosts of other days inside.

Not until she died would that door be opened again.

She engaged a room at a local hotel. Then for 35 years Ellen MacDonald maintained her chauffeur and a caretaker for the grounds of the old house.

Almost daily the little woman would ride out and inspect the grounds, give sharp orders to the caretaker and return to her lonely room. Every winter during those 35 years, the caretaker kept a fire in the furnace, but was not allowed to venture upstairs. The house was a sepulchre.

One cold March day, the day maid found Ellen had passed away in her sleep, and proper authorities were notified. A brother came from New York to see to the funeral arrangements, and was not a little surprised to learn of the old homestead and what had happened.

This writer was allowed to roam through the house a few days before the contents were to be auctioned off.

Long years of darkness had turned the whiteness of the massive woodwork to yellow, the once beautiful drapes, the filmy curtains and the rich carpeting all were faded and falling apart.

On one side of the great living room stood an old Chickering piano with its red upholstered stool. I touched the keys and a discordant note pierced the musty air. Spread all around were glass globes, under which old-fashioned wax flowers lay, discolored with age and falling in decay. Pictures on the walls in massive frames, beautiful vases, dishes and silver, priceless furniture and a fortune in fine old linen, lay covered with inches of dust. Cobwebs hung from corner to corner and draped over the throw pillows arranged on the old settee, like fine tatting lace to hide neglect.

In the high-ceilinged kitchen was an old-fashioned sink, a range and clockshelf filled with old remedies, denoting life had once existed. On the table were the remains of a 35 year old breakfast. The coffee pot containing powdered grounds still rested on the stove.

Hesitating before going up the winding cherry staircase, I seemed to be treading hallowed ground. As I stood at the bottom of the stairs, I could imagine how the beautiful Ellen must have looked as she stepped slowly down to greet the man who, a few minutes later, was to be her husband. Perhaps the wedding march was played on that dusty piano in the corner. I waited for the phantom Ellen to pass, and then ascended the long, easy staircase.

Upstairs all was silence. The thick carpeted floors made no sound, as I tried to feel what perhaps Ellen Douglas MacDonald felt as she walked through those rooms — the loneliness of silence.

In the front bedroom, Ellen's room — something small lay on the floor near the window. It was an old Valentine, frilled and colored. Wiping the dust from the design of red hearts and forget-me-nots, I found these words, "May This Little Gift Bind Thy Life With Mine." Could this little faded love symbol have had anything to do with Ellen's loneliness?

Tomorrow men would come and carry away the beautiful dishes, the pictures, the priceless furniture, the sterling silver but they would never know the happiness nor the disillusion that these articles had been through. The drapes and rugs would be burned. They were of no more use and it is right that it should be that way.

The legend of Ellen Douglas MacDonald will live in Oxford for many generations.

There are those who would call her eccentric, but when one peeps behind the curtain that had come down over a life that had been rich in promise, he comes to only one conclusion.

She was lonely.

AN INVENTION IN GUILFORD

Age is no barrier to genius, and some God-given talent may crop out at any time in both old and young. A great writer has said that every man has had, at some time of his life, an original idea that could have made him great, but many thousands of these ideas are lost in the world because they are not used.

The story of Elsworth Phelps, a young 16-year-old boy who lived in Guilford, in Chenango County, in the years following the War of 1812, brings out this point, and is a story of one who grasped at his idea and gave it to the world.

Elsworth Phelps was not a "long hair". He was just an ordinary kid who went to the little log schoolhouse near Guilford during the winter months, and did chores at home morning and night. Like other boys of that time he was slated to be "bound out" to learn some trade when he became older, or else he would take over the family farm, but neither of these things interested young Phelps.

Records are vague on Elsworth's parents but when he was 16, he lived with the Hon. Samuel A. Smith in Guilford. Without a doubt he was a musical prodigy, but with nothing to guide him except his own intuition. From the time he fashioned his first willow whistle in the spring, he was interested in musical sounds. He made larger whistles with deeper throats and more musical tones, and then began to build them with different tones. Using his jackknife he whittled off just the amount of wood needed to change the tone. Soon he had fashioned sufficient pipes to run a double chromatic scale, each tuned to the finest degree of accuracy.

With unmatched genius young Phelps contrived a way to put these pipes together in sequence and to manipulate them with valves operated with keys. How many times he had to tear down his work and start over, no one will ever know, but finally the first organ was finished and its notes were a balm to the tired boy who had struggled to bring them to life.

When the new organ was built, a crude affair to be sure, word of it was sped eastward by the stage drivers and

41

travelers. Promoters and investors came to Guilford on horseback to see the new instrument.

Money was soon available, and the wide-eyed Phelps, with no money of his own, was persuaded to sell his interest to others. He was retained as voicer and tuner, and a factory was set up. The first organ made there was sold in Oxford.

Like many other great discoveries, the Phelps organ was soon copied. Factories grew up in New York and other large cities where materials were easier to get, and the little Guilford factory began to lose money.

Another young man as poor as Phelps had come to Guilford with the idea of using lead pipes and together they rolled lead to almost paper thinness, making each pipe a little different size, and were surprised at the result. The tone was sweeter than with the wood pipes. This discovery stimulated the little factory for a time, but the distance to the source of the material was too great.

The end came when the larger organ makers began to copy the lead pipes, combining them with the wooden ones for difference in tone. Today the great pipe organs all over the world are made of both wood and lead pipes.

Finally the little Guilford factory had to close its doors. Phelps went to New York, where he obtained work in one of the large factories.

Those for whom he worked waxed rich, but Elsworth Phelps plodded along, making great improvements, for which he received neither money nor credit.

Today, as the majestic pipe organ peals forth in the great cathedrals of the world, few know that many of the ideas involved in their making came from the genius of a Guilford boy who today sleeps in some forgotten cemetery in the metropolis, unknown and unsung.

"BUT SIR, HE'S MY BROTHER"

"For greater love hath no man than this, that he lay down his life for his friends."

This statement of holy writ has many times brought a feeling of peace to the hearts of bereaved families, when someone had given his life to save another. But it never did mean so much to the people of the community around Norwich as when spoken one Sunday afternoon by Chaplain Harrison W. Foreman as he stood before two open graves in the South Plymouth Cemetery.

Men who give their lives to save others are called heroes, but when a brother gives his life in a vain attempt to save a brother, the story takes a sacredness that is never forgotten.

Herman Bennett was 24 and had just returned from service in World War I. Behind him lay many adventures and narrow escapes, because during the war he had seen plenty of service and much death. Tired of war, he was happy as he kissed his parents, Mr. and Mrs. Herbert Bennett, at the old Lackawanna station early in June, 1919. He was now ready to embark on a new life where war would be no more. Little did he know where this last adventure would lead.

Herman's brother, Herbert, 21, was employed at the ice house of E. J. White on the Springvale Road, a mile east of Norwich. In June the ice pond, where winter harvests of ice were made, was a calm warm body of water just right for swimming.

On June 12, 1919 Herbert Bennett and Clifford Frink were working in the ice house, getting a load ready for delivery around the city, when Herbert saw his brother Herman coming up the road toward the pond. All waved gay hellos and Herman went into the bushes and emerged ready for a dip, on this hot muggy day.

Although he had bathed in the pond hundreds of times before becoming a soldier, he was not a swimmer.

Herman waded around, calling at times to the two young men at the icehouse, who called back little pleasantries in return.

43

Suddenly Herman threw up his hands and disappeared beneath the surface. When he broke surface again, he called for help and the two men in the icehouse ran around the shore to the place Herman had been. Peeling off his clothes, Herbert jumped in, forgetting that he was not able to swim either. He grabbed his brother, and then both disappeared beneath the water.

Young Frink, who could swim, was in the water trying to rescue the brothers who were locked in each others' arms. Frink tried a dozen times to reach them and finally just made it to shore before his own breath gave out. Several times he plunged back in to search the bottom, but the brothers were gone.

Frink then called to Ward Lewis and James Goodrich who lived nearby and all three began to search for the bodies. Finally, Mr. White, the owner was contacted and he ordered the sluice opened and the water drained from the pond. The sluice was opened, but there was still about ten feet of water in the pond, when Goodrich saw the bodies and plunged in and brought them to shore.

Two doctors tried in vain to restore life through artificial respiration. The large crowd that had gathered was silent and finally the doctors announced the young men were both dead.

The bodies were taken to their home in South Plymouth, and met by a sorrowing family and a host of tearful neighbors.

The following Sunday the largest funeral ever held in the little hamlet took place, with the unusual sight of two hearses drawn by white horses, leading a hundred carriages to the cemetery.

Chaplain Foreman told the story of another sacrifice of many years ago when another had died to save many. He read the immortal words given at the beginning of this story.

Again, they brought comfort to the sorrowing.

THE GODDESS OF JUSTICE

Standing atop the Chenango County courthouse in Norwich is a likeness of the Goddess of Justice, carved out of wood from the forests of Chenango. No one really knows how long she has been standing on the dome of the Hall of Justice, but it is thought that it must have been since the stately courthouse was built in 1837. Today few can recall any unusual circumstances surrounding that image of the goddess. Old timers though, still shake their heads and solemnly attribute some strange "goings on" to the supernatural. Perhaps Fate did voice disapproval of something that had occurred inside the stone walls.

Like a lady in a somnambulistic trance, the Goddess of Justice stretches forth her right arm as if looking for something she cannot find, while her left arm is raised high above her head holding the scales, symbolic of the justice that lay within the ponderous doors of the courthouse.

When the builders placed the scales in her hand they were thought to have been securely fastened. But the builders did not reckon with Fate.

In 1862, exactly 25 years after the courthouse was built, a citizen was brought before the bar of justice. There was doubt among the townsfolk that he was guilty, but after a trial the jury found him guilty and sentenced him to prison. Although the populace was stunned at the verdict, there was nothing to be done. The following day a phenomenon took place that startled the natives. The scales in the hand of justice were dashed to the ground!

After a year they were returned by an enterprising steeple-jack, who climbed the dizzy heights while a crowd below cheered. There they remained for 14 years and in 1877 they again were missing. Men climbed to the parapet, but the scales had disappeared.

That was the year the late Judge W. F. Jenks was campaigning for office.

One October day Judge Jenks was speaking from a platform stretched out from the courthouse steps. A large crowd had gathered to hear what the politician had to promise. At the end of his windy speech, he declared, "Reelect me and I'll-I'll--" The judge was lost temporarily for words.

"Restore the scales to the hand of Justice!" a wag yelled from the crowd, amid snickers and guffaws.

"Yes, that's it," the judge laughed. "I'll restore the scales to the hand of Justice."

The promise became a byword and the good judge was reelected. Then came another surprise. The day after election the missing scales reappeared on the courthouse dome, swinging again from the hands of Justice! It was later revealed that the scales had been brought from an attic in New Berlin, and this gave voice to two explanations.

First, that the scales had been kept as a souvenir. The second, and supposedly most likely, was that the scales were not the original scales at all, but a similar pair from another Goddess of Justice in some other town. Be that as it may, two young men with ladders had come at dawn the day after election and had placed the scales in the outstretched hand. It is doubtful whether the old judge knew the whereabouts of the scales at all.

It was just three days after the execution of the hapless Felix McCann, in June, 1879 on the lawn of that same courthouse, as a circus parade was passing, that a deputy sheriff was looking out of a window in the Sheriff's office, directly across the road from the gallows. Suddenly there was a clanging sound as the scales of Justice dropped to the ground directly on the spot where the gallows stood!

Had McCann been wrongfully executed? He had pleaded guilty to shooting his neighbor, over a chicken. But he admitted to being drunk at the time, not knowing what he was doing. Should the governor have granted the new trial that McCann's lawyer had begged for?

In 1892 the scales again fell and were lost. For two years the lady stood with an empty hand outstretched. Then one day a gang of painters discovered them wedged in the parapet below the feet of the Goddess. They were replaced and supposedly secured for all time to come.

Since then the scales have fallen and have been restored intermittently, no matter how well they are fastened.

In 1948 the scales became missing. Miss Justice held aloft her empty hand for two years, until in 1950 when the building was painted, the scales were rescued from the parapet again and returned to the waiting hand.

For some time the Lady's right arm was missing. It had fallen off and become misplaced while awaiting a brave steeple jack to replace it. This problem was overcome when the sheriff hired a local craftsman to duplicate it. By taking a picture of the Goddess's shadow on the ground, he was able to determne the size and shape of the hand of justice. This work had to be done by hand, but every curve and finger is perfect, and reaches forth as if pronouncing a benediction.

The lady still looks over the valley, with the hand of justice pointing to the east. The winds of almost 140 years have blown about the wooden skirts of her majestic presence, and the sun of as many summers has beaten against her head — but she stands firm, as a symbol that all men are created equal and should have equal justice.

THE SMITHVILLE FLATS STORY

If a Revolutionary colonel hadn't failed in business in his home village of Litchfield, Conn., and in discouragement plunged into the woods of New York State, the history of the Town of Smithville, in Chenango County, might have been vastly different.

Today, Smithville Flats, although a small village, lies in one of the prettiest spots in the state, a land of beauty and fertility surrounded by the green hills of Chenango County. The area is rich in tradition and at one time was a most important place, geographically and historically.

But to get back to the discouraged colonel. It was back in 1788 following the close of the war, that the troubles of one Col. Epaphras Sheldon began to close in on him.

The dashing officer had resumed his business after the war, only to find that the instability of money made business next to impossible. He kept on, getting deeper in debt each year, until finally his creditors closed him out. He is said to have been jailed for his debt and after serving his time was unable to face his neighbors.

History tells us that Col. Sheldon said goodbye to his wife and children, packed a knapsack and struck out into the wilderness. In those days everything beyond the Hudson River was "the far west," and many who had set out never came back. So it was with many tears and misgivings that the Sheldon family said goodbye to husband and father, never expecting to see him again.

Colonel Sheldon kept on, aided in direction only by the stars and sun. Finally, tired and starved, he halted to rest in the valley of what is now Smithville. There, by chance, he came upon a hunter, Robert Lyttle, an Irishman, who had erected a shanty near the river. Lyttle, a roaming fellow, told Sheldon of the wonders of the country and the game that abounded there.

The Colonel began to clear some land and as the summer waned he decided to carry the news back to his friends in

48

Litchfield, before the winter snow locked him in among the hills.

Late that fall a bedraggled man reached Litchfield. The whole town turned out to see him and throughout the winter the townsfolk listened to his story as he told and retold it in the tavern. To a neighbor Joseph Agard, the enthusiastic traveler painted a glowing picture, with the result that Agard and his family agreed to accompany Sheldon and his family back to this Garden of the Gods.

It was the summer or early fall of 1798 that the two families finally reached Chenango County. The hunter, Lyttle, had gone leaving his cabin deserted. In it the two combined families, comprising 15 people, moved, but it was soon found that someone must get out. According to the Agards, this crowding was just too much and they decided to start their cabin, even though winter had already set in. They started another cabin and before the roof was on they moved in. The family huddled together, keeping warm with a roaring fire built in the center of the floor of the "pen". Often in the morning the cabin would be half filled with snow.

After a most terrible winter, spring came and the two families planted small patches of corn, completed the Agard cabin and began to live. That summer other families from Litchfield came and soon the present Smithville Flats (named from a Dutch settler named Smith) became a settlement, with a trading post on the river.

The third year the first wedding took place, when Evas Bragg, a stalwart young pioneer, won the strikingly pretty Roxy Agard. Meanwhile another settlement was started further downstream by Edward Loomis, who had moved from Oxford in 1799. Loomis eventually opened a road from Smithville to Oxford, a road still in use.

In 1813 the original Baptist church was organized but it wasn't until 1825 that it was finally built. Then in 1826 the edifice burned to the ground.

Many said at the time that the reason the church burned was because of the actions of some of its members. It seems that the Smithville Flats church was the offshoot of a church in Greene that had split because it's pastor and some of the

49

members had joined the Masonic Order. The future prosperity of the church, after it was rebuilt by the generosity of the Agard family, discounted this theory.

Capt. John Palmer kept the first inn and the first store, coming to the Flats in 1806. He also had the first distillery. By that time the settlers were coming in faster and already several dozen families had erected cabins. Palmer did a good business, but in the staples and fire-water line. The first school was taught by Samuel Askeel, who came among the first settlers. Askeel, a stern and efficient teacher, taught the 3 R's to both whites and Indians alike.

Thus, adversity in one part of the nation was the seed of happy and peaceful prosperity, in another part. Col. Sheldon, by the stint of hard work and integrity, prospered in the new land and was instrumental in bringing more and more easterners to the fertile valley.

In his old age, he became homesick for the East and went back to Litchfield, leaving the others to carry on the colony he had founded.

THE LOST OPERA STAR

A newspaper man in search of a story sometimes runs into a veritable gold mine, and makes new friends as he seeks to find a story as he treads the sidewalks of a city in search of material for a waiting Sunday edition. Often the mere blowing of a straw in the wind will disclose a story that may set the world agog and furnish the solution to a mystery that had long been given up and probably forgotten.

Such was the story of Edward Oden, a world renowned operatic singer, whose talents at one time earned him the recognition of being the world's greatest basso, an artist sought after to sing before the crowned of the world, an artist who shared the popularity of the inimitable Caruso and those other greats of the operatic stage. Edward Oden walked off the stage one night following a performance and was never heard from again in the world of opera.

Fate has a way of causing events to come to pass, often in simple and unexpected ways, and when the pieces begin to fall together they take on the appearance of belonging that way, and the passing of years serve to add to the romance of such an occurence.

Let us go back more than a score of years to a warm spring day in Norwich. This writer, a reporter for a metropolitan newspaper, was walking along the street in search of a Sunday feature story. I was new to the town and had been sent to Norwich to "cover" for an expected replacement. As I walked along in the sunshine, I passed a small photographic shop, which seemed also to be the home of the photographer. I had experienced difficulty with my press camera and wondered if perhaps this photo studio owner might set me straight. I knew no other photographer in the city, so decided to go in. I was greeted by a pleasant woman, who said that her husband was in the developing room at the moment and invited me to be seated.

The walls were covered with various enlarged photos and the one which attracked my interest was a picture of a handsome man with an attractive "goatee", a picture that seemed to be that of Mephistopheles, in the opera "Faust." I soon became lost in that array of greats which faced me as I sat in the studio.

Then the door opened and the photographer entered and put out his hand. His smiling face was vaguely familiar. I had seen it somewhere.

We conversed on several subjects and finally mentioned music, a topic in which I was vitally interested. My new friend also expressed a similar interest.

"You are a musician?" I asked.

"Yes," he replied, as one recalling something far away and sweet.

"Yes," he again whispered, "music was once the greatest thing in life to me."

As a reporter, I felt I was on the verge of opening a door that had been long closed. The man's wife became slightly agitated. He was gazing at the floor. I glanced at the photograph on the wall. I felt that something wonderful was about to happen.

"Edward," the lady whispered, "perhaps we have talked enough. Maybe we had best come back to the present."

Was this to be the end of some long kept secret? I was becoming as excited as one would feel had he just stumbled onto a gold mine!

Would one be doing the right thing in breaking down the barriers of the past in order to give the world a story? Was I doing the right thing in helping this man to get a nightmare off his chest? My senses told me it was a very personal, almost sacred thing he wanted to tell.

Then he started to speak, "It has been 35 years," he said. "I believe I have kept that secret long enough. Yes, I want to tell you. I feel that it may bring peace after all these years."

The wife smiled as though in agreement. She, too, seemed tired. She had seen her father lowered into his grave without knowing his daughter's secret. Was it now to be revealed?

Yes, he had been in show business. The photographer seemed to be on home ground. In fact he had been with Raymond Hitchcock, he said, not as one would boast, but casually as though reminiscing. Indeed, he was reminiscing, for 35 years had come and gone since Raymond Hitchcock was one of the great stars of Broadway.

I listened with rapt attention as the photographer mentioned great names, told of studying in Italy, talked of great roles. Certainly no one but a man of extreme popularity could have known these people, and no one but an artist could talk so understandingly of such mythical giants as Faust, Mephistopheles, Don Carlos and others. Somewhere back in my mind a thread of recollection persisted. We had not even asked each other our names.

"What did you say your name was?" I asked.

"Edward J. Odenkirchen," he answered.

The skies cleared in my mind a little, "Would you be the long-lost Edward Oden, the artist who disappeared from the concert stage so many years ago?"

The photographer nodded, "I was Edward Oden back in those days," he admitted. "That was 35 years ago. My real name is Odenkirchen."

The reporter could scarcely grasp the thrilling significance of that moment. He had discovered the man for whom the great Caruso had searched — discovered him plying the trade he learned while studying in Italy. The story of Edward Oden reads like a tale from a storybook.

Born in New Haven, Conn. the boy early discovered that he had a good voice, and as he grew older that voice developed into a beautiful basso. Friends urged him to study, so he began to work under Batteli of New Haven. Enthusiastic over the accomplishments of his pupil, Batteli advised him to go to Italy, there to study under the world renowned Bussini.

The lad journeyed to Italy and under the new teacher advanced rapidly and his exquisite voice attracted the attention of Enrico Caruso. So impressed was Caruso that he took the young basso in tow and the two toured Italy together, sharing the billing. Then they parted, Caruso to come to America and Oden to continue his studies.

When the time came for Oden to leave Italy, he faced a situation common to young artists. He was broke. He went to the American consul who agreed to help him. Indeed, he would

53

give the budding artist a journey home he would never forget. He knew a sea captain and the captain would gladly take care of the matter.

When Oden was put on the boat by the consul, the captain welcomed him. Directing the young man to follow, the captain started downstairs. The downward flight continued until the pair had to stop. They had reached the bottom of the boat. In one corner lay a pile of shovels.

"Take your pick," the captain ordered. "You are shoveling your way across. Now get started."

For a month the young man, who was later destined to be billed as America's Premier Basso, shoveled coal and slept on a pile of boiler grates, until finally the Statue of Liberty held up her welcoming arm to the tired and blistered voyager.

In New York City success awaited him. His first booking was with Henry W. Savage's production, "The Student Prince." Others followed and the young singer worked long and hard. Despite warnings, he continued at a fearful pace, burning the candle at both ends, giving all he had to his career.

Then it happened. A doctor said he detected something seriously wrong with the ambitious singer. He would have to slow down or he wouldn't live much longer. Oden didn't tell anyone of this prediction, but he stayed until the booking date expired.

Finally the last night came. As the audience cheered on the other side of the curtain, Edward Oden knew that it was his last curtain call. He walked slowly to his dressing room.

Without bidding any farewells, Edward Oden went out into the night and walked to the railroad station. He hadn't even picked up his pay at the theater. Going to the ticket agent, he laid $4.51 on the counter, asking for that much transportation on the next train out.

When the conductor touched his shoulder a short time later, he looked out to see a small Adirondack village. One he had never seen before. This was as far as his money would take him. It was also the beginning of a new life.

A little later he knocked at the door of the village doctor. Perhaps seeking a remedy to ease some pain. Little did he know that the pleasant young woman who answered the door, would become his wife and the mother of his two sons.

He closed the door to the stage, to the life of music and glittering costumes. He opened his heart to seek joy and peace from the simpler things.

With the woman who happened to be there when he was called upon to make a great decision, who brought to his life the only cheer that was possible, in such a crushing situation, Edward Odenkirchen came to Norwich and opened his little photography shop. Over the years he had nights when he was awakened by the strains of an orchestra. Those who urgently sought him passed on, one by one. His escape was nearly complete.

Thus Edward Oden remained obscure, alone with his memories, until a reporter brushed away the cobwebs from the door that the world's great had long sought in vain.

THE BIG WIND AT BEAVER MEADOW

Faithful Sons of Erin still reckon time from the "year of the Big Wind in Ireland," but few know that a wind stronger than anything Ireland or any other country has ever produced, once hit the hamlet of Beaver Meadow and for two solid hours blew across Chenango County.

There is no one alive today who can even faintly recall that hot July day in 1833 when the wind suddenly blew across the southwestern part of the county, and blew toward the northeast, following a path exactly a mile wide across the townships of German, Smyrna, Pharsalia and Beaver Meadow, blowing itself out in Madison County.

Details of the great blow are vague and the few available facts are contained in an old record now faint with age owned by John Gregg, now of Chemung County, whose ancesters lived in Chenango County, near Beaver Meadow.

We will try to piece out the story from the scrawled record in an ancient "copy book" handed down to Mr. Gregg, himself, nearing 80. Mr. Gregg has filled in the chinks missing from the story by recalling recitals of the story from his father around the family fireside at North Beaver Meadow, a settlement now omitted from the map.

It was a hot, humid day, so close that the men had to stop haying. It was difficult to breathe and all one could do was to sweat and hope for the coming of the night and cooler air. The horses were unhitched from the wagon, and stood under the lea of the barn switching at flies which seemed to dig deeper on that terribly hot day.

Suddenly, about 4 o'clock, the sky darkened. Then a stiff breeze came up, stronger and stronger. The horses began to grow fearful and raced toward an open field, their harnesses dragging behind them. The cattle had been under the trees in the orchard and suddenly they sprang to life and ran toward the open field, where the horses were headed.

The wind was growing even stronger by the minute, and it looked as though nightfall was prematurely upon them.

The barn started to waver as parts gave way and scattered lumber all over the yard. Small buildings collapsed as if made of cardboard. The poultry in the yard couldn't control their flight and were blown every which way, losing feathers and squawking with fear.

The men and boys ran towards the woods, the women coming from the house to follow. The trees around them nearly doubled down to the ground, but there was no where else to go. Some of the forests were toppled like matchwood, killing the animal life by crushing it.

Most of the farm houses, substantially built of huge timbers, withstood the blast, although many roofs were lost. Barns, chicken houses, and other poorly constructed buildings were destroyed. As far as is known no lives were lost among the people.

In the adajacent neighborhoods the sun shone throughout the blast and only a mild breeze fanned the remainder of the county. When the storm was over, the people from the other side of the hills could scarcely believe what had happened. They saw the desolation in the one-mile strip. It seemed like a nightmare.

It took a year to rebuild the barns and to repair the homes. Some never were replaced or repaired, but many "bees" and "barnraisin's" were necessary before the farming could be resumed in the now-famous "one-mile-strip."

Perhaps meteorologists could explain the Big Wind of Chenango in 1833 if accurate data were available, but whatever the reason was the phenomenon has never recurred.

For years the old timers ran for shelter at every stiff wind, fearing a return of their terrible experience.

Today, many of the rebuilt barns still dot the countryside from German to Smyrna, and all of them are braced with huge oaken braces strong enough to withstand the next tornado that comes this way.

THE CHAPMAN AND TURNER BUILDING

One day nearly a century ago, a 14-year-old boy got off a packet boat on the Chenango Canal at Norwich and got a job in the W. L. Scott planing mill, which stood where the Berglas Manufacturing plant is now. The boy had already learned the carpenter trade and it was not unusual that the shop foreman set him to making four mortar hods for a stranger. That was in 1875 and the boy was the late Melvin Kemp. The new building on which the hods were to be used was the Chapman and Turner Building that long stood on the corner of West Main St. and South Broad. For many years the four story building was the largest department store in Chenango County.

To many the Chapman and Turner building was a landmark. Although somewhat old fashioned in architecture, with its front entrance gained by steps, the building became so well known to native Norwichites that it became an institution.

Before this magnificent building came into being a rather ramshackle wooden store and a residence stood on the site, and it became an eyesore to the proud merchants across the street. It may be a revelation to some to learn that the wooden house that once stood where the great Chapman and Turner building was, is still in existence and houses several families at 19-21 Fair St. The beam construction shows no signs of deterioration and the house, although moved on rollers and planks to the Fair Street address nearly 100 years ago, is still plumb and true.

Under the date, April 8, 1875, the Chenango Union carried a note about the moving of the house which was purchased by Oliver Dimmick, then it continues, "work upon the new block to be erected by J. O. Hill & Co. will commence in earnest."

In the fall of 1875 the excavation began and in the spring the actual building began to rise. The construction of such a large building caused considerable talk in the community, and "board walk" engineers were as much in evidence then as they are now, when a new building arises.

From an old yellow clipping dated February 26, 1876 comes this bit of information concerning the building.

"J. O. Hill & Co., dry goods dealers, have finished and will occupy the 1st of March as fine a brick building as most cities can boast of. The structure is five stories high, with French roof and tower. Dressed stone trimmings, pressed brick, pointed with dark blue cement, have been used in the construction. In the tower is to be placed a clock, which will be illuminated at night.

"The basement is large and well lighted, the excavation extending under the sidewalk. The first floor will be used as a general salesroom. In the second story a liberal space has been allotted to the dressmaking department. Col. E. J. Loomis and District-Attorney Knapp have rented offices on this floor. A suite of rooms has also been rented to Miss Robinson, of Pitcher, who will carry on dress-making business.

"The entire fourth floor will be used as a carpet room, and the fifth for storage purposes."

Thus the biggest building to be built in the town was erected. It came at a time when the people were proud to point out the progress of their merchants. Factories had sprung up and the railroads were coming into their own. The common workers seemed flush with money and this was before taxes had to be instituted.

Some time later, Wm. H. Chapman & Co., already in the dry goods business bought the Hill block and took in a partner, J. B. Turner. Together they did a flourishing business for several decades. The building contained the first elevator to be installed in Norwich, and it was still in use when Urban Renewal demolished the building in 1968.

Without a doubt many stories could come from the citizens of Norwich about their experiences in the Chapman & Turner building.

Many parents took their children in just so they could ride on an elevator for the first time. Many remember that queasy feeling as the slow cubical rose between floors, and the sudden sinking feeling as it came back down!

The original clock in the tower, with its four sides telling the same time for all to see, was wound by a chain with weights on each end. It had to be wound once a week. Various officials of the store personnel took turns doing this and sometimes someone would forget, then confusion reigned on the streets until it was going again. Then one day the old clock, nearly 25 years old, refused to keep going. Its gears were worn out. Norwich had the same time for over 30 years after that!

In 1932 a new electric clock was purchased by the Ladies Village Improvement Association. Mrs. Lena M. Flanagan was president of the society, and the group agreed to make the clock their foremost project. When a holiday ball failed to net enough money, Mrs. Flanagan and Mrs. Wm. Reed Turner solicited residents of the city, selling minutes on the proposed clock at $5 a minute. In less than 2 days they had raised $850 and the clock, with a unit for chimes, and a unit for a broadcasting set-up, was purchased from IBM by a committee, comprising of Frank Zuber, Melvin Eaton, Mrs. James Kent and Mrs. Flanagan.

Another story that comes from the old building was told by one of Norwich's dearly beloved citizens, the late Henry Gabler.

It seems that Henry was at the time a gas meter reader. He had read the meters on the third and fourth floors of the large store and had come down to the second floor, carefully fastening the stair door behind him. Just as he was about to descend the stairs to the first floor, there was a terrible racket on the stairs and a cow — yes, a cow, was galloping up, all out of breath with sparks flying from her nostrils! There was Henry trapped in the upstairs hall and the beast was coming on! The entrapped meter reader made a dash for the nearest office door, the door of Dr. Harris. At that moment the doctor's door opened an inch and a wild-eyed patient looked out, slammed the door and turned the key.

Across the hall the door of Judge Sullivan opened a few inches and when the judge saw the cow making for the door, he too, slammed it shut and locked it, leaving Henry to his fate. The fact is that the judge didn't see Henry.

The door of the dentist, Dr. Switzer, also opened a crack and was immediately slammed and locked.

Mr. Gabler said he didn't know how he ever escaped the horns of the infuriated beast, but he knew he climbed walls and posts that nobody ever climbed before. The human fly had nothing on Henry balancing himself on the picture molding.

However, George Follett, who had been driving a herd of cows to the train when the ugly one had made a break for it, raced up the stairs, tackled the wild bovine, throwing it like a wrestler and roping it tightly. The cow was then skidded down the stairs and into the street, minus the hide on its left side.

Henry, his legs feeling as if they were made of rubber, went back to the office and took the rest of the day off.

The building has also known tragedy. In 1954 Mr. and Mrs. Frank Hendrickson took refuge in their parked car at the curb on the West Main Street side to wait out the winds of Hurricane Hazel. At the very height of the storm a section of the cornice gave way and came crashing down upon the Hendrickson car, killing both occupants.

When the old building was condemned and Urban Renewal demolished it, Norwich citizens felt they had lost a friend.

THE TRAGEDY OF HANNAH COOPER

Standing on the side of the road, between Gilbertsville and Morris in Otsego County, is a monolith surrounded by a stout iron fence. To the east lies a long and beautiful valley backed up with panoramic hills, on the other side of which is Oneonta and the valley of the Susquehanna.

Delving into the history behind the lone monument, one uncovers a story of heartbreak and romance, long since silenced by the ages. For on this very spot, nearly two centuries ago, a beautiful young girl, the sister of James Fenimore Cooper, met death in a fall from a horse.

The story of Hannah Cooper is told in various ways. Hannah was the favorite daughter of Judge William Cooper, a staunch Quaker settler who came from Burlington, New Jersey in 1790. He settled on the shore of Otsego Lake founding the community of Cooperstown. Hannah was one of 12 children, and according to tradition and contemporary writings, was "talented, beautiful and good."

Hannah lived with her father while he attended sessions of Congress in Philadelphia, and had many friends and admirers. Among her friends was one whom she, in turn, admired very much, a son of Gen. Jacob Morris. He lived in the famous old Morris Manor, a great mansion that still stands on the Gilbertsville-Morris road. It is still occupied by descendents of General Morris.

On Sept. 10, 1800, Hannah, who had just turned 18, and one of her brothers, either William Jr. or Richard (James Fenimore was only 11) started from Cooperstown on the 24-mile ride to the Morris home. The ride was through valleys and over hills, almost entirely through woods in which Indians roved. Frontier families in those days were in daily contact with these denizens of the forest, so Hannah and her brother had no fear on that score. Hannah, perched in a side-saddle, with her long riding skirts nearly touching the ground, made a pretty picture, as the autumn sun glinted through the trees.

As the pair came within a short distance of the Morris home, Hannah wanted to change her pony for the spirited mount of her brother. She wanted to ride the new Arabian steed her father had purchased for her brother, in order that she might make a better impression on her beau. Her brother tried to reason with her. The Arabian had never carried a side saddle, nor had he ever carried a long-skirted woman. The brother knew the horse was tired but by the convincing manner of his sister he finally relented, deciding it would be safe for her in the short distance they had left to go.

The saddles were changed and the boy helped his sister to mount. As they were about to start toward the Morris home, a dog ran from a farmhouse and frightened the Arabian. Hannah was thrown from the horse, striking her head. She never spoke again.

The brother turned about when he saw his sister was dead, and rode back to Cooperstown with news of the accident. Judge Cooper and Moss Kent, another admirer, and other members of the family started at once for the scene, a long and silent ride.

Hannah was taken back to her home and laid on the old Queen Anne table, (now the library table at Otsego Hall in Cooperstown) later to be laid to rest in the little family cemetery.

A year later, the monument which now stands on the side of the road was erected by an unknown admirer on the very spot on which Hannah Cooper met her fate.

A final chapter of the story of Hannah Cooper is called by some historians, "the graveyard romance," and disclosed that another admirer of the hapless girl was dashing Col. Richard Cary, a friend of Hannah's father. Just before the gallant Virginia Colonel died he whispered to his mourning family that he had one last request.

"Bury me beside Hannah Cooper," he said. "She was the best woman I ever knew, and my only chance of Paradise is getting in on her skirts."

This was a shock to his wife and family, but they respected his wishes and buried him where he still lies — close beside the beautiful Hannah Cooper.

OPERATION HUMANITARIAN

The night seemed especially dark as a large bus rolled up to the Norwich Township Grange Hall and came to a halt on the frozen snow.

When the bus door opened a half dozen frightened faces peered out into the below-zero darkness. First one man stepped from the bus platform, and then another. They were in a strange land and entering upon a new adventure.

Immediately a score of people ran from the lighted hall. Upon each was pinned a large cardboard badge reading, "I speak Hungarian." The committee that greeted the haggard refugees began to call out cheery hellos and at the sound of their native tongue the Hungarians responded. When all 41 of the new guests had alighted from the bus and had obtained their luggage and other worldly goods, most of it tied up in cartons and in valises furnished at Camp Kilmer, N. J., they were ushered into the warm hall.

To the Chenango County people assembled at the Grange Hall that night, it was one of the most emotional scenes they had ever witnessed. It seemed that every American realized that here among them were people who were homeless, tired, hungry, and fearful. But it also seemed that the one who "tempers the wind to the shorn lamb" was also there.

As the refugees, some with small children in their arms, entered the door into the hall a loud cheer went up and a hundred clapping hands thundered a welcome. The people who represented America to the strangers then went to the visitors to help them off with their wraps, to hold the babies, and to smile the welcome they could not speak.

There was no language barrier that night. A warm handshake and a smile meant more to those refugees that night than a thousand words. It seemed that the tears of joy from those homeless people told a story more beautiful than any ever heard in any pulpit. Here was Christianity in action. There was no room for religious differences. Everyone seemed to sense the presence of Him who looks into the heart, and the heart alone.

As the visitors were about to sit down to a warm supper prepared for them, Ray Whitlock, one of the leaders in the project, played a recording of the Hungarian National Anthem. As the first strains of the hymn rang out the startled group came to attention. One young woman buried her face in her hands, while tears began to trickle down the faces of others. Soon they were singing — these people who had scarcely dared to sing a few months ago — and the men looked resolutely upward as the words of their sacred anthem rolled through the building. Gone was fear. Gone for the moment was heartbreak. They were at last free and this hymn seemed to be one of gratitude. Truly it must have seemed good to them to hear their own hearts singing, even though the words came through streaming tears.

This was the introduction of 41 Hungarian refugees to Chenango County, where they had been brought on that night of January 16, 1957.

To many it must have seemed as it did to the children of Israel, thousands of years ago. They may have murmured as they were taken to the bus, but now the Red Sea had been crossed and they were in the land which would henceforth be their home.

The project to bring the Hungarians to Chenango County had started less than two weeks before, when suggestions had been made over the local radio station that some of the available jobs, some of the homes, and some of the generosity available should be offered to these heartsick people waiting at Camp Kilmer, N. J.

When Mayor Adelbert Button of Norwich called a meeting to discuss the matter, the response was immediate. Some 70 people, many of them leaders in the community and embracing three faiths, attended.

Rev. Avery Post, a Congregational clergyman, was named chairman of the meeting and the mayor named committees. He stated plainly that no one present had ever been connected with such a project before, and no one knew exactly how to proceed. But, he said, there must be faith with which to offset the lack of experience. The cause was good, therefore the committee would surely be guided to do the right thing.

Work began the following day. The radio and the newspapers told the story. The housing committee began to list available apartments and rooms. No one knew how many would be needed, but they were listed anyway. A local merchant donated the use of a large vacant store and an efficient housewife offered her time in taking care of the business of accepting used furniture, clothing, money and other articles for use in the project.

Donations began to come in. Money came from all sources — money to be used to pay the transportation charges and for use of the refugees until their first paychecks came. Only $1,000 had been asked for. No one knew how much would be needed, but when the donations were counted the quota had been doubled. There was more than enough for the present needs of the new people, and any that was over was turned over to the Red Cross Hungarian Relief Fund.

The day after the refugees arrived work interviews started, with willing interpreters on hand to assist the New York State Employment Service interviews. There were more than enough jobs — work that no one else seemed to want — but the Hungarians accepted any kind of job with gratitude. They knew they were here to become Americans and were anxious to get started. No American lost his job because of the Hungarians, although unthinking persons started rumors to that effect.

The following Sunday every refugee attended divine worship. They were unable to understand the service, but they came — each to the church of his faith, and each certain that his prayers of gratitude were heard no matter in which tongue they were spoken. To many it was their first opportunity to worship in a church atmosphere in many months.

Some months later a member of the staff of the State Employment Service, accompanied by an interpreter who was himself a refugee, called on as many of the Hungarians as they could within the day. They talked with both employer and employee. There was complete satisfaction all around.

New York State's Governor Averell Harriman, impressed by the result of Chenango County's experiment named the project "Operation Humanitarian," and well he might. The work was carried out, not for personal gain or for personal praise, but with the thought of brotherhood and love.

"Inasmuch as ye have done it unto one of the least of these, my brethren, ye have done it unto me."

GO-WAN-GO INDIAN PRINCESS

The bustling village of Greene in Chenango County was not always the busy community it is today. It is filled with ghosts of the past — some of these of ravishing beauty, such as the Indian Princess, "Go-Wan-Go," a beauteous circus performer and daughter of an Indian doctor who lived in Greene over a century ago.

It is the story of the glittering spangles of circus days, and also of tears of unhappiness, grief and loneliness which seem to appear even to those who seem so undeserving of this pain.

Carrie Mohawk was an Indian girl, the daughter of Dr. Allen Mohawk, who dispensed his Indian remedies from the little brick cottage still standing on one of the main streets in the village. Princess Go-Wan-Go, as she was known to her public when she became the toast of circus goers as an Indian rider, was hailed for her exquisite beauty as well as her ability in the saddle.

Dr. Mohawk and his wife, Lydia, came to Greene before the Civil War. Lydia was a young woman of considerable beauty and grace and made a decided impression on the villagers. The doctor and his highly educated wife, kept much to themselves, and did not push themselves upon the residents of the village. In spite of this, the good doctor's practice grew and his remedies were accepted by the residents of the village. Although there were two other physicians in the village, Dr. Mohawk received his share of patronage.

Dr. Mohawk was an avid horseman. In those days horses were the sport of those who could afford to own a fast animal. A story is told of a challenge issued to Dr. Mohawk by a new resident of the village. No self-respecting horseman would ever turn down a challenge to race. A date was set and the track lay on the site of the present Greene Central School.

In the meantime the wily herb doctor had learned in some manner that the horse to be pitted against him was a former horse-car horse of considerable speed. Unknown to anyone,

68

Dr. Mohawk installed a large gong under the body of his racing cart and the race plans were made. The two horses were started and near the end of the last heat the doctor reached for the cord and pulled it. The gong blasted out and the poor horse-car animal, remembering that such a gong was a signal to stop, pulled up so quickly that it almost threw the driver over the dashboard. Dr. Mohawk's horse crossed the line for the victory.

There was considerable controversy, but nowhere in the rule book could be found a law against putting a gong on a racing cart. The crafty old doctor collected the money, and gave the village something to chuckle over for a month.

Meanwhile the doctor's pretty daughter was growing more and more beautiful. She became a familiar sight as she rode her horse at top speed over the fields and roads outside of the village. Her beauty and riding ability attracted the interest of the owner of a large circus and Princess Go-Wan-Go was offered a place among the top performers of the day and she accepted. Her success was instant. She became one of the best and the most attractive girl riders in the business. Because of her Indian extraction and her fresh natural Indian beauty she soon became the toast of the circus world.

The manager of the show was a dashing young man with a strange name, Captain Charles Charles, who had been a cavalry officer in the Civil War. He fell madly in love with the beauteous Go-Wan-Go and the two were married. Later, with money saved from their salaries they started their own circus unit. Their success was phenonomenal, and both stars rose high into the zenith. Princess Go-Wan-Go and her horse, named Buckskin, became known the world over. Life was a pleasant melody for the happy couple who had come to live in a new world — a world of spangle, glitter and flickering torch lights of a circus. They prospered and were loved all over the world.

It didn't seem that anything could ever come to end such bliss. But one is not always sure of the future.

Shortly after the new show had reached these heights through the grace and beauty of the girl rider, grief came. Captain Charles Charles was stricken suddenly and by the time Go-Wan-Go reached his dressing room he was gone. She had just finished her act under the big top and while taking her bow amid the terrific roar of applause, she was told to come quickly. But as Fate would have it, she was too late.

Go-Wan-Go, weakened by the death of the only man she had ever loved, fell prey to a serious illness. To add to her troubles her favorite horse, Buckskin, had an accident and never recovered.

Beaten down, but not vanquished, Go-Wan-Go tried to go it alone. By that time illness and the years had taken their toll of her beauty, although her spirit was ever young.

Finally she had nothing left but memories — memories that haunted, yet shone like stars over her past. Her trunk filled with circus clothes was all that remained of those days when the world was at her feet.

No one knows much of Princess Go-Wan-Go's final years, but one day in 1924 word reached Greene that their favorite daughter had gone. She is probably buried in Edgewater, where her mother spent her last days.

In the village cemetery a large monument marks the resting place of Dr. Mohawk. This and the little brick house, now occupied by a prominent Greene family, are all that is left of a saga that will live forever in that little village in Chenango County.

THE GOLD CURE

Alcoholism was almost as much a problem before the turn of the century as it is now. It was before the days of Alcoholics Anonymous; it was before the days of the "shock" treatment, and it was before the days of the tantalizing liquor commercials — tantalizing because if a hapless individual is trying to free himself from the bonds of the liquor habit, those appetizing pictures flashed across the nation often cause him to abandon any endeavor to break the chains.

It was back just after 1890 that this very fight with liquor actually put Norwich on the map. To hundreds who wanted to be cured of drunkenness, Norwich seemed to be the answer. It was in Norwich that the world-famous "Gold Cure" was located and where it continued for about 30 years.

The Gold Cure was a more or less fabulous institution where men (it was mostly men at that time) could come for either a temporary or permanent cure, or come as a boarder to get himself "evaporated" after a prolonged bout with John Barleycorn. So popular was the "Gold Cure at Norwich" that men from the whole country made a beaten path to its door. Doctors of that time praised the institution as "upstanding" and after only six months of operation there was a large number of "graduates," and of these only a few returned to their cups, so the story goes.

The Gold Cure Sanatarium, now the site of East Main Street School, was operated by one Philo Aldrich, starting in a large house on the site. Men began to come or were brought in all conditions. Some came by themselves, remorseful and staggering. Others made arrangements in a business-like way through the mail and came from long distances by train. Many cases were sent by police and still others came for no other reason than to "sober up" before going home. People seemed to have faith in the "Gold Cure at Norwich."

Philo Aldrich had developed a process that brought drinkers to their senses by injecting a substance known as "bichloride of gold" into the veins of his patients four times a day for three weeks. At the end of three weeks a test was made which consisted of giving the patient a big drink of whiskey. He was invariably made severly ill — often to the extent that he wanted to die, and in a few hours he would be recovered completely and the desire for liquor was gone.

Then for an entire week the man was put into his room and whiskey left conveniently near, but few ever touched it. When the desire for drink was actually gone — and according to reports of Dr. Aldrich, this was usually the case — and the patient felt sure of himself, he would be discharged. Most of the patients never returned.

The Gold Cure Sanatarium was managed with efficiency. A dozen pretty and competent nurses flitted around, with no more than ten patients to one nurse. The sanatarium was staffed with two highly trained physicians who watched each patient constantly.

"Dr." Aldrich (and there is some question as to whether he was a medical man or pharmacist) in a lecture delivered some years ago, told a group of his fellows that when a man left his "cure" he was through with being a slave to drink. The future was before him but he could, if he wished, build up a new appetite or he could leave it alone.

Some of his patients unfortunately renewed their acquaintance with liquor after a few years of freedom, and this went far toward damaging the reputation of the sanatarium at Norwich.

The sanatarium had a private wing to which wealthy and prominent men were brought from all over the country. This wing was a money-maker for Dr. Aldrich, but the service given to these men was no different from that given to the poor fellow who had just been picked up in the gutter the Saturday night before.

There is no record of the reason why the Gold Cure closed. Whether the bichloride of gold compound was not good for humans, or whether business fell off because of the few failures, is not known. About the time of World War I the building was taken over for use as a large boarding house, and then purchased by the school district in 1922.

There has never been anything detrimental or shady said about the reputation of Dr. Aldrich or his institution. Indeed, it had been written up in most of the medical journals of that time. It is thought by some that the excessive cost of the cure may have been a factor, although Dr. Aldrich did not grow rich.

Be that as it may, the Gold Cure may have failed, but the deeds of one man to rid the world of one of its worst demons should not go unnoticed.

HOLMESVILLE ON THE UNADILLA

The population of Holmesville in Chenango County back in 1880 was 168. Today a count of noses would reveal a few less, perhaps. Yet 90 years ago Holmesville was a busy center.

Back in the days when it took nearly a half day to drive to the nearest village, Holmesville was one of the countless little settlements along the highway that meant a great deal to the farmers. Farmers in the Unadilla Valley did their trading in the small villages instead of driving to Norwich or Oneonta as they do today.

In the sleepy little hamlet on Rt. 8, where now not a wheel of industry turns, there once stood two stores, a saw and shingle planing mill, a grist mill, a cheese factory, two boot and shoe shops, a blacksmith shop, two wagon shops, two cabinet making concerns and a cooper shop. The church and school are still there.

Where are all of these industries?

For a village of 168 people a lot of work was done and Saturday night in Holmesville was as happy as a Saturday night in Norwich or Oneonta is today. Farmers waited until Saturday night to go to the village to do their trading. Some of them took that night to stop at the hotel to get a snort or two to ease up their old war injuries, and enjoy a friendly social time.

Saturday night was farmer's night and Holmesville was a farmer's town. Their simple needs could be purchased there and a store keeper was not averse to taking in a few dozen eggs to help pay for Willie's shoes or flour, sugar, gingham or cut plug.

Waterman Fields built Holmesville's first store in 1833. His father came from Rhode Island and took up land about two miles west of New Berlin. His son Waterman did not have the urge to push a plow or do the other hard farm work necessary to wrest a living from the soil. His father objected to Waterman leaving the farm, but nonetheless he left to become a merchant. Surprising his family, the son became a success in his little store in Holmesville, well liked by the friendly folks and honest in his dealings.

Grist mills were described as so many "run of stones" and the mill at Holmesville must have been a large mill for history tells us it contained "three run of stones." It was propelled by water drawn from the Unadilla river by means of a ditch, a quarter of a mile long, affording a fall of six feet. It was built by Mason White, the ancestor of many families of that name who still live in the vicinity.

Hundreds of tiny villages like Holmesville still dot our countryside. Now mostly residential, they all boomed with business and activity during the horse and buggy days.

Once a busy shopping and manufacturing center, the hamlet of Holmesville in Chenango County is now entirely residential and its population hasn't changed in nearly a hundred years.

DISAPPEARANCE OF WHAUPAUNAUCAU LAKE

Nobody knows how long ago it was. It may have been a century or two ago. All that is known about the disappearance of Whaupaunaucau Lake is that the lake existed in the fertile valley where the road twists and turns and finally disappears in the Whaupaunaucau hills to the east of Norwich.

Legend tells us that one night a terrific roar was heard by Indians camping on the shore of the lake and that the water began to lower. After an hour or two there was a loud sucking noise as the water from the lake gurgled down into the earth, leaving nothing but a few small ponds and many dead fish to mark the spot. The once sparkling blue body of water, played on and in by Indian boys with their father's canoes, had completely disappeared!

There are many legendary stories about the lake that vanished that summer night so long ago. One of these is about the Indian with a toothache. It seems that the Indian was in great pain from an aching molar. During his agony he was tormented by the crying of a new baby that had been born to his squaw a few days before. Finally in desperate anger he grabbed up the infant and threw it into the campfire. A short time later the lake disappeared.

Another tradition tells of a bride of a young Indian brave, who was drowned in the lake a few days before the lake vanished. In this case it was thought that the Great Spirit was leading the doomed girl to the Happy Hunting Grounds. The body of the dead girl was never found, which was proof that the girl had reached her destination.

It was a number of years after the lake had vanished and the stench had subsided, that the valley began to show signs of renewed life. But to the Indians it was bad ground — haunted ground.

Somewhere floating around in the dark caverns left when the water coursed down into the earth were ghosts — ghosts that were pretty real to the superstitious people with the ability to see them. It seemed natural that the cry of a wildcat should be mistaken for a scream for help from a young drowning bride, or that the whimpering of fox whelps could be mistaken for the cries of a burning babe.

Over the years the benighted savages became more brave and began to seek game in the valley. Those who had witnessed the disappearance of the lake had passed on to their reward leaving behind them a legend that was not to die so easily.

For many years hunters forsook the valley which had become a place of entrancing beauty. There were ghosts in that valley all right. Echoes came from the many caves hidden in the valley, echoes that could only be the voices of those who had lived there before. Echoes that could not be stilled. The Whaupaunaucau hills were to be avoided, except by the wild animals. The bear, deer, wolves and panthers had a sanctuary all to themselves.

Then one day a hunter, stopping for the coming winter, on his way "West" decided to roll up a cabin. Unknown to him, he had picked a spot in the most dreaded part of the valley. When others saw that he was not disturbed, they came and built cabins also. History seems to agree that no one knows how long ago it was that the lake was sucked down into a great hole about halfway up the valley, never to be seen again. There have been minor floods when water raced down through the Whaupaunaucau valley due to spring freshets. The fact that these freshets never seemed to find the way out once used by a glimmering lake many years ago is puzzling to conservationists even today. There is clear evidence that such a lake once really existed. But only legend gives any clue as to what happened.

Did the Indian father who so cruelly destroyed his own child really anger the Great Spirit? Did the young Indian bride cry out for deliverance as she sank beneath the waters of the shimmering lake?

Whaupaunaucau Valley still lies in the spring and summer sunshine. The fertile soil grows good crops and the trees stretch their arms to the sky.

The hunter of today still walks silently through the forest paths, often imagining that he can hear the scream of a baby or the soft sound of someone following him.

A number of secluded farm homes now stand silently on the winding lane-like road up through the valley. The ghosts of the past seem to have hovered out of existence, leaving only the landmarks of days long gone.

THE RAILROAD COMES TO NORWICH

The first DL&W depot at Norwich was a wooden building, modern for the times. It had spreading eaves over the space between the door and the tracks to protect the passengers from rain or snow as they alighted from the trains. It was a thrilling sight to see one of those trains puffing up to the station, the engineer leaning out of his cab, the lord of all he surveyed. Few could understand that this man was actually getting "paid" for riding on such a magnificent monster, which obeyed his every whim.

Around 1900 the present building was built. The original station was torn down and the ornate building, approximately 100 feet by 50 feet, with its pagoda type roof was constructed. Built of native hand-chipped stone, it was ready for use within a year. The day the first train stopped at the handsome new station it was greeted by Johnson's Band. For many years it was known who purchased the first ticket from the window, but this information has been lost.

The railroad brought business and entertainment to Norwich. It was a beehive of activity. Theatrical troupes unloaded and loaded at the depot, and horse-drawn cabs took the theater people to the Eagle Hotel on North Broad Street. Their stage fixtures were hauled in wagons to the Breese Opera House, located in the present Masonic Building. In those days Norwich was known as a theater town, and most of the finer shows and musical troupes played in the old opera house. On show nights cabs would bring the more well-to-do of the city to the theater in style, and this era continued until the movies replaced this form of entertainment in theaters all over the nation.

Circuses also unloaded and loaded at the DL&W yards, and many a lad has shivered in the early morning air watching this wonderful sight. Farmers brought milk, cabbage and other produce to the depot, and hundreds of coal cars were unloaded each year. Salesmen, widely known as "drummers", came by train and put up at the hotels, hiring rigs from a

79

local livery stable to go to other towns that were not on the railroad lines. Tramps rode the rods, and many a night the local police station, just across the tracks, was filled with smelly knights of the road.

According to police of a few years ago, the police station was always busy looking after the wanderers who sought accommodations for the night. It was said that two local bakeries usually furnished day old buns for the use of the hungry guests.

Norwich soon became popular with these knights of the road because of the food furnished every morning, but the bakeries continued their practice as an outlet for surplus stale products. Then it is said that this excellent service finally spelled the doom for the hoboes, who gathered in ever widening circles much to the chagrin of the taxpayers.

Finally about the time of the passing of the vagrancy law, this generosity was halted. An immediate falling off of visitors was seen.

But before this happened most every over-night visitor brought with him a bundle of newspapers. These were used to place under and over him as he slept on the hard floor of the police station. Promptly at 6 in the morning, the police station would be emptied of its guests for the night, and aired out, ready for the next batch of homeless men.

At one time it is said that 14 passenger trains, containing 5 or more coaches rolled in and out of Norwich in a single day, besides the freight trains, circus trains and others. It soon became big business for horse drawn omnibuses to travel from two stations, the O&W, near the eastern edge of the village and the DL&W in the center of town.

Norwich boasted of several large hotels at that time and many people profited from the railroad coming into the town.

Then one day a solitary, home made truck drove into town. This particular vehicle did not mean more than an oddity, but it portended the end of rail travel and rail freight hauling. It also meant the end of the line for many great railroad men who seemed to love their work.

Soon other trucks were made and it was found that freight could be delivered faster in many cases by trucks, and that folks could ride more conveniently and comfortably in automobiles.

But the railroad passenger service did not die easily. It continued through the years as the revenue grew less and less. Better coaches were provided and better services offered, but the handwriting was on the wall. In 1951, the last passenger train left town, never to return.

During World War II a number of Norwich people were employed at the Scintilla plant in Sidney, doing defense work. The O&W took many coaches out of the moth balls and ran several shifts to Sidney for this purpose. Also troop trains were established and both railroads were transportation for foreign prisoners of war on their way to American prison camps.

Today the remodeled depot, still convenient and picturesque, belongs to the city. The tracks upon which once ran the majestic passenger trains and puffing locomotives are now used to move freight for the DL&W. Instead of the huge steam locomotives, the cars are moved with deisel engines, which ply back and forth with a silence that seems foreign to old time railroaders.

The O&W, which once served the valley is already gone, and its tracks are torn up. A big modern high school occupies the former freight yards.

The old order changeth, "the bell and screech of the steam locomotive whistle is no longer heard in the land."

GAIL BORDEN WAS BORN HERE

The story of Gail Borden is one of unhappiness and frustration. A native son of Norwich, who is lauded as the pioneer in processing milk, was born Nov. 9, 1801, in a small house that stood on East River Road, just north of Hawley's corners. Gail Borden, after almost a lifetime of frustrating work, did finally obtain patent rights. It is said that other patents had been stolen from him, and it was not until he was 55 years old that he was really able to strike out for himself.

When Gail was a very young boy the family moved to Texas where Gail actually grew up. He is said to have produced the first topographical map of Texas, and later to have designed the city of Houston.

He also was appointed port collector of the city of Galveston. At this time he was well known for his political ideals and did much to strengthen the ties of Texas. He helped run a newspaper with his brother, Thomas, and supported the revolt of Texas against Mexico, about 1835.

Regardless of all the important positions and acclaim he received polictically, there seemed to be an urge he couldn't forget, an urge that haunted him. How could milk be processed so it could be shipped to distant points, for millions of babies and others who had no milk?

Although he owned 14,000 acres of land, and raised cattle besides all his other interests, the thought kept nagging at him.

In those wild days, still remembered because of the massacre at the Alamo, Borden started in earnest to perfect a milk product for army use. He first made a meat biscuit for use by the army which was also used during the Civil War. This product was the forerunner of the famous K-Ration.

His friends of that time said that he was so involved in the manufacture of these things that he neglected to patent them, not thinking that anyone might cut in on his patriotic work. But people are not always generous, so Borden drifted close to bankruptcy.

His credit went down also, but he was determined to perfect a milk product. His experiments took much time and money but he was confident there could be a method that would preserve milk.

The result of losing his patents only served to spur him on. He made friends with a lawyer, who was able to obtain funds and Borden now fully protected, began to manfacture condensed milk and brought out a product that could be sent overseas, even in the slow sailing ships of that day.

He had little money but his product became well known and there were plenty of men willing to buy stock in the Borden Company. His first factory was established in 1856 at Torrington, Conn. The product came into great demand and other factories were built in various dairy sections of the country.

One was built in Norwich, and the street on which it was built was named Borden Avenue. The mammoth building was finished in 1900, and young Floyd Wood, a Norwich farmer's son was the first to draw up to the new Borden plant to deposit the first load of milk to be made into Borden products. Radzell Aldrich, a prosperous Plymouth farmer, was the first farmer to sign a milk contract with the company.

Young Wood stayed up all night so he could be the first one at the plant when it opened on that cold day in January. It was still dark when he whisked his father's team and bob sleigh out into the snow-chocked highway and headed for the condensery. Just behind him were other farmers, all anxious to be first, but the boy with the bay team grinned victoriously as he helped to unload his cargo of fresh milk.

The plant contained seven large boilers and an 80 horsepower Corliss engine and one pump. Workmen were still on the job getting in the finishing touches the day before the plant opened. Supt. Frank Enos breathed a sigh of relief, as they finished. He had promised the farmers that the Borden condensery would open January 14, and he aimed to keep his word.

Two days after the first load was delivered, the first batch of milk was completed. This was a plain unsweetened product, with no keeping qualities, and had to be used within a week or it spoiled. It was put directly into stores and sold in bulk. Most of this first product was shipped to New York to be sold from door to door, and was the forerunner of our present evaporated milk.

While one gang of men were unloading milk at the plant, another crowd of men were cutting river ice from the Chenango River, which ran within a few yards of the plant. It was stored in two large barns on the property. When these barns were filled, a huge stack of ice, 40 by 80 feet, was built on the site of a proposed new icehouse. The house was erected over the pile of ice, so that it was enclosed. The company was fortunate that year, expecting to have to haul ice into the plant from other sources, when a sudden freeze started at the end of December and the river froze to 11 inches thick. This furnished enough for the summer and also gave employment to many men whose normal work was idle in winter. That year over 1500 tons of ice were cut and stored for the condensery.

The Borden Condensery handled milk for over 50 years, but finally transportation and assembly line methods progressed to the point that the Norwich plant was no longer needed. Later the Victory Chain, a local grocery wholesale establishment bought the building for their business.

In 1957 a monument was erected at the site where Gail Borden was born, donated by the Norwich Township Grange to commemorate a century of condensed milk manufacture, using Gail Borden's discovery.

Gail Borden's final years were devoted to the things he had always wanted to do. An ardent Baptist, he helped establish Baylor university, the largest Baptist college in the South. He was spared only 15 years in which to reap the reward of his life's work, and died in his beloved Texas in 1874.

When young Borden looked across the Chenango River from his shabby little home he didn't know that some day a huge milk processing factory bearing his name would stand there. Nor that it would be an important factor in the economy of Chenango County, bringing employment and security to hundreds of people.

McCAULLY'S PLIGHT

In November and December as the Christmas crowds surge back and forth along the main thoroughfare in Norwich, few will realize that one of the prettiest and most heart-warming stories in Chenango County took place on what is now the site of, or nearby Frair's Gift Shop.

Ebenezer McCaully was one of the group of New Englanders who came to central New York in the days which are now in the very early history of the state. McCaully was a wild sort of character, kind and considerate to his family in his way, but very undependable. He was sort of a Rip Van Winkle type and often and without notice would take his gun and be gone as much as several weeks at a time. Where he went on these excursions was not known, but his wife was accustomed to his actions and got along the best she could with the children, knowing that one day the errant husband would return, penitent and apologetic.

It was just before the year 1800 that the McCaullys arrived in Chenango County. Some believe he worked for Capt. John Harris as a surveyor's helper, but there is no record of that in history. He was evidently a roustabout, working only when he had the inclination or to keep his family from starving.

The story goes that one day Ebenezer took his gun and started for the woods, which were then surrounding the tiny settlement. It was a warm September day just right for a man to bring a brace of pheasants home for supper.

By October he had not returned and when November snows began to fall, the wanderer was given up for dead. The widow huddled her children around her and prepared for a long, cold winter, with only such food as the neighbors saw fit to bring in.

November wore on and then came December and its deep snows. The young widow McCaully had taken a few jobs, nursing the sick and helping out as a mid-wife. In spite of her courageous efforts, the children were undernourished and she, herself, had all she could do to keep going. Severe sickness visited the frail little ones and their mother believed that by spring all would be gone.

The dark skies of December grew darker as the month waned. It was nearing Christmas, but this meant little to the tired forlorn family. There was no Santa Clause in those days, but the Christian folks of the settlement had compassion. They helped all they could from their own meager store, but the spirit of the season seemed insufficient that year. They were unable to help the widow who was waiting for her brood to die.

It was nearly midnight on Christmas Eve, and without hope for a merry holiday the family had wrapped themselves in quilts and gone to sleep.

The scraggly dog lay by the hearth catching the last heat from a fading ember, when he began to growl. Someone was coming. The hair on the dog's back began to bristle, and he started to bark. This aroused Mrs. McCaully and she waited with baited breath. Then the dog's tail began to wag and a loud "hullo" rang out. Throwing off the covers, she ran to the door. When she had unbolted it, she saw her husband standing there! He stood tall and straight with his gun in one hand and a deer slung over his shoulders!

The story ends there, as far as meager records go. Some think that the man had gone as far as Fort Stanwix and he might have been imprisoned on some minor misdeed. No one will ever know, nor does it matter.

When Avery Power's family died, it is thought the McCaullys went in a wagon train with Power to the West. Although records do not mention them again, they were a part of the great westward movement looking for peace and prosperity in our fabulous country.

WINDSTORM IN A CEMETERY

As a rule the numerous cyclones and windstorms visiting the area of Chenango County are few and far between, in fact this part of the country should feel very fortunate, compared with many other vicinities that are devastated almost annually.

But this account of one of the worst storms ever to hit Norwich, occurred June 15, 1889, causing more damage in fewer minutes than any known storm before or since.

It was a close humid Saturday, and life in Norwich was at a standstill. The funeral of Paul Westcott wound slowly along Broad St. towards Mt. Hope Cemetery, just south of town. Aside from that there was little activity in what was usually a busy street.

As the cortege reached the open grave the preacher began to read the committal service. In the west a dark cloud appeared and a breeze came up. The coolness was welcome, but soon the group around the grave began to get apprehensive as the cloud over the hill grew blacker. It appeared to be a thunderstorm in the making.

The minister hastened his service and pronounced the benediction. The group dispersed and teams and carriages left the cemetery hurriedly. The sexton, Mr. Foster, also became alarmed and without filling the grave, hurried for his nearby home.

Suddenly a terrific windstorm tore down from West Hill, leaving a swath of uprooted and broken trees in its wake. It surged along toward Mt. Hope cemetery, leveling everything which came into its path. Houses and barns were crumpled and carried away. Stacks of early June hay were scattered for miles.

Striking the cemetery at the northwest corner the cyclone tore through the once quiet city of the dead. Huge monuments began to topple and fall as the wind bore down. Suddenly it changed its path and plowed northeast, across Canasawacta creek, uprooting big trees and destroying much of the east side of the village. Then it took an easterly course and spent itself on the Francis Grant farm on East Hill, leaving a path of destruction never before seen in Chenango County.

The storm stopped as abruptly as it had started and a pelting rain soothed the raging wind and cooled the atmosphere. Then the sun came out and calm returned to the earth.

When a list of the damage was compiled it was found that 28 monuments and 38 headstones had blown over. The huge shaft marking the grave of Dr. H. K. Bellows had been turned around on its pedestal. The 12 foot shaft of polished marble over the grave of George R. Day had been lifted several feet into the air, hurled a dozen feet away and was plunged top-first into the earth, embedding itself about two feet. The monument weighs several tons. Fortunately it was not broken and was restored to its base.

Many of the monuments were broken beyond repair and still remain a memento of that terrible June afternoon.

Excepting the tornado which swept through Beaver Meadow many years ago this is said by old timers to have been the worst the county has ever seen.

There are still many who recall that famous storm of over 80 years ago and those who remember still tell of the fear that gripped the people for those terrible few minutes.

THE GUILFORD CENTER CHURCH

One day, back in 1801, a young minister from Oneida rode horseback to the tiny settlement of Guilford Center, with an avowed purpose of preaching the Gospel to a Sabbath-desecrating community. Guilford Center was on the early stage route through Chenango County and to the south, and was still inhabited by wild animals and a few straggling Indians.

The Rev. Israel Brainard held just one meeting in the old school-house, where he preached a fiery sermon against the evils of breaking the fourth commandment. What happened at that meeting will never be known, but the good reverend returned to Oneida and it was a whole year before another service was held in the little schoolhouse in Ives settlement.

During the next few years traveling preachers held meetings and exhorted the settlers to repent, but it was not until Deacon Samuel Mills moved into Guilford Center in 1807, that religion began to fall in quantity upon the community. Deacon Mills was a tough old Christian, and from the time he arrived, he refused to loan his team to a group of Sabbath breaking men. Religion began to burn in the hearts of the householders.

Today the work started by the good deacon back in 1807 is still progressing in the little white church at Guilford Center. In all of the years since the church was built in 1817, there has been no lull in the work. There have been many ministers who have been proud to preach at Guilford Center since its inception.

During the past century the little white church, still in perfect repair, has prospered. In the basement are facilities for the church suppers, wedding receptions and the like.

For many years the church has been the scene of a great Harvest Supper in October. The fare consists of turkey and all the fixings.

Except for its modern furnishings, the auditorium is the same as when it rang with hymns started with the old tuning fork in the hands of the village schoolmaster.

When modern folks begin to wrangle over small church differences, they would do well to pause and read back into history. Today, few congregations are faced with the job of church building, for on the most part the churches we use today were built many years ago, except for a few new projects.

An example of real Christian fortitude and stalwartism is wrapped up in the story of the Guilford Center Church. Many were the troubles and problems which had to be surmounted before the church was established. Poverty, disease, discouragement and want all contributed to the hardship of building the temple wherein all men of all faiths might worship God.

In June, 1816, sufficient lumber had been cut from the woods with which to make the frame. All winter the men worked in the woods getting out logs for the adz-men to form into timbers. In those days the adz was the principal tool in erecting a frame and there are few men today who can use the outmoded instrument. With it they squared the logs to size, ready for the raising.

It took several days to raise the frame of the church, but all helped. The men came early, just after chores, and worked hard until noon, when the women served dinner in the shade. Then they worked until chore time. This went on for five full days, and then the frame was ready for the carpenters. By late fall the building was finally enclosed. Then the money ran out.

With the church partly built, the good people met in the schoolhouse, as they had been doing. It was three years before they decided to brave the elements and use their church, which was without lath, plaster or ceiling. A carpenter's bench was used as a pulpit, and planks stretched across saw-horses, served as seats. In the winter there was no stove for a long time. The pastor preached from his bench with his great coat up around his ears. Still the people came, determined to use their church.

There is a truism written somewhere that "God tempers the wind to the shorn lamb" and these stern heroic Christians had occasion to test that truth. From somewhere came one of the scarcest articles of that time, a stove. So new and "modern" was this stove that it took a special meeting of the congregation to "admit" its use in the church. It looked sinful to some of them, but they were won over and thereafter worshipped in more comfort.

Before the seats and pulpit were built a great revival swept over the community and converts swarmed to the church, adding 71 new members. This was taken by many a demonstration of the Almighty, for of themselves, they had little to offer the new members. But with the aid of these converts the church was finally completed in 1820.

As if to further test the faith of the congregation, the town was swept by a fatal fever, taking many of its members. On the heels of this some of the people withdrew to form another church at Van Buren's Corners, but the faith of those who were left remained steadfast. When it seemed the blackest the tide began to turn and folks flocked back to the church, bringing others with them. So great was the influx of members the church had to be made larger, and in 1855 was dismantled on one end and 10 feet added.

Today, over 150 years since the frame was raised, the church at Guilford Center is still thriving. The obstacles that harrassed the early builders have been overcome by steadfast work and faith, and posterity is now reaping the benefit of their labor of love.

One old timer whose grandfather was one of the original members, said recently, "In those days folks depended on God and they knew that if they did their best for Him, He would help them. That church was fashioned by the hand of the Almighty, and I don't look for it to disintegrate."

COLONEL LOOMIS AND HIS CHENANGO LAKE INN

There was probably no more colorful personality in the history of Chenango County than Col. Edwin J. Loomis. There are still many today who will remember the old host of "Colonel's Inn" at Chenango Lake and may have had a part in some of the incidents about to be related.

Colonel Loomis was a local leader in this part of the country ever since the days of the Civil War. When the war broke out the colonel was almost 13 years old, but big for his age. He easily fibbed as far as 17 and was taken into the service and made a name for himself at the battle of Port Huron. It was not until later however, and after the war had ceased that he was dubbed "Colonel". This was a political gift bestowed because of his activity in politics around 1862 when the "greenback" was introduced as the currency.

Colonel Loomis was always colorful. He is said to have been the most civic minded person that Norwich has ever had. The Loomis original home stood on the site that the YMCA now occupies on North Broad Street. In his drive to beautify the city he gave the band pagoda that still stands in East Park. Although somewhat modernized in recent years, it has seen many public gatherings and concerts besides being a "home away from home" for Santa Claus on his yearly visits. The bandstand was erected in 1878, nearly a hundred years ago.

In 1880 Col. Loomis got the idea of having an inn on the shore of Chenango Lake and straightway set about building it. Always one to act on the spur of the moment, the Colonel put a score of men to work and the building was soon open for business. It was a mammoth three-story affair nestled among the trees adjacent to the main road and on the lake shore.

Some men have the Midas touch and can be a success anywhere.

Such a man was Col. Loomis. Because his food was the best in the state, crowds flocked to Chenango Lake. Fresh fish, caught from the lake; home grown poultry and vegetables and plenty of roast beef, lamb and mutton. His guests never got up from the Colonel's table hungry.

Louis Starr of Norwich, who as a boy actually caught the fish that were served at Colonel's Inn, tells how patrons came with teams from miles around to dine at the Inn. The Colonel's cook was Mr. Starr's mother, who could prepare lake fish and eel in a manner that brought customers back every Sunday. The colonel delighted in serving eel to those who were squeamish about them, without the patron knowing he was eating eel. So palatable were the eels that many kept ordering the "Rocky Mountain Trout" even after learning that they were nothing but lake eels.

Mr. Starr tells of catching 400 to 500 perch in a few hours, using a half dozen poles on the dock. The perch were skinned and plunged into ice water. They were then dried between towels, dipped into batter and fried in deep fat like friedcakes. When done, the fish came to the top of the kettle and were served piping hot. Colonel's Inn perch were known all over the state.

July 4, 1882, was said to have been the biggest day the county has ever seen. Colonel Loomis advertised a big Fourth of July celebration, hired three bands, arranged many games and attractions and loaded his larder with scores of roasts of beef and many other foods. He was taking a long chance, for if the day turned out to be rainy, he stood to lose hundreds of dollars in food alone, as there was no refrigeration in those days.

By noon of the Fourth teams were tied to every tree in the woods along the road for a mile. Folks came from Syracuse, Ithaca, Cortland and Utica.

Many left their homes the day before in order to make it. To the Colonel's delight, it turned out to be a lovely summer day. Old timers figure that there must have been 40,000 people at the lake, but this may have been exaggerated. However they came and they stayed. There were fireworks all night from a raft in the middle of the lake and hundreds of people remained all night, sleeping on blankets in the woods,

93

or on straw in the wagons and carriages. The Colonel made a fortune that day.

On June 18, 1918, Colonel Loomis died at his home at the Inn. He was only 73, but a long illness had sapped his strength. He was a 33rd degree Mason and his fraternal friends came from far and wide to pay their respects. Besides that the city turned out. It was a funeral in keeping with the Colonel's character, and one the like of which has never been seen in Norwich since.

POLKVILLE
The Name That Wouldn't Change

Some villages acquire their names in unusual ways. Some are named after writers, soldiers and even race horses, depending upon the person or persons who named them. Most of these names stuck, but in Chenango County there is a hamlet that was originally named after a great president and then had that name changed to a more modern cognomen, only to have it changed back again to the name that residents insisted upon calling it — its original name.

Polkville is not a big place by any stretch of the imagination, but it has a tavern and is the location of Norwich's grange hall, town garage, town hall, the county's SPCA and a dozen or so residents.

But Polkville has a story that dates back to 1844 when James Knox Polk was running for President. Up to that time the little hamlet had no name, but it had a number of lively inhabitants. It seems that at that time Polk was advocating the annexation of Texas to the United States. So were the brawny men of the little four corners in the middle of Chenango County.

There were fights over nothing and the more men that stood up to the tavern bar at night the bigger the fights. All that one had to say was a word against the presidential candidate, and he would become the center of a free-for-all. It became a fever.

The story goes that a ladies group had decided upon a name for the little settlement and this didn't sit too well with the men of the place. They had decided, and loudly so, to name the place "Polkville" after their hero. While no families were broken up, there were many arguments between husband and wife. Something had to be done about it and soon.

Then it happened. The presidential election rolled around and John Knox Polk was still a candidate. It was time the settlement had a name. Over in Norwich, a mile and a half away, a big parade had been planned. The men from the settlement decided to join it, and on parade night a large crowd of farmers and workmen from the settlement marched with lighted torches to the village of Norwich, intending not only to parade but to march into every store, church meeting or any other gathering they found and to announce the name of their settlement by calling out, "Polkville Forever!"

They did just that, but they also imbibed at all the Norwich taverns. There were fights and more fights, but still no one knew what they were fighting for. But they had succeeded in bringing their message. The name "Polkville" stuck, probably because no one wished to mention the name proposed by the ladies.

Finally the name of Polkville was officially placed on the map and business went on as usual. The battle was soon forgotten, and with the election of Polk, everybody was happy, whether they cared about Texas or not.

Polkville was never a thriving place, but it was home to a number of people, mostly farmers. The brawny citizenry of yesterday had passed on, as had their hero when the county board of supervisors decided to give the settlement another name. It was called "East Norwich" and was so designated on the maps and signboards. While this was accepted, probably because no one really cared, the remaining old timers found it hard to make the change. It was still Polkville to them. Somehow nobody could remember the new "East Norwich."

A few years ago a town truck pulled up to the corners, two men jumped down from the cab. They walked to the back of the truck and pulled off a new sign to put in the hole where the old East Norwich one had stood.

In large letters it read POLKVILLE.

THE BIBLE GUARDS A MILL

If the old limestone walls of the present "Stone Mill" in Norwich were to be torn down stone by stone a small mortared crypt in the three-foot thick wall would be disclosed. If this crypt were broken into, an old Bible, probably decayed and yellowed with age, would be revealed.

But let us begin the story when it actually occurred back one August day in 1836.

The story is that one of the masons working on the building was a convert to Christianity after having done much evil in his community. One night the man's little son was dying. The lone doctor in the settlement could do no more. It seemed that only a miracle could save the fever ridden child. The boy's mother called a minister to offer the last rites to the dying child. As the kindly Reverend stood by the boy's bedside, the child's father staggered in, drunk and angry. He berated the minister for coming, for after all if the good doctor had failed to restore the child to health, what did a preacher think he could do?

Suddenly, as if pushed down by a mighty hand, the intoxicated man dropped to his knees. Filled with fear as he viewed the almost lifeless little body, he promised the Almighty that if his son's life could be spared he would henceforth dedicate his life to Christianity.

By morning the fevered child was sleeping peacefully and the fever was somewhat abated. Today's doctors might say that the fever had run its course, but the distracted father knew it was his sincere promise that had saved his son. The father did his part, he gave up drinking and became a convert to religion.

Although the name of the converted stone mason is now long forgotten, the man's life was transformed. He asked for and received permission to implant a Bible somewhere in the thick walls of the mill, believing that it would bring success to any work performed henceforth in the building.

97

That was 150 years ago. The crypt holding the Holy Book was known only to those who assisted in building it and its whereabouts is no longer known. Someday, sometime, another workman, engaged in tearing down the old mill may find the spot, formed by the trowel of the convert.

This story came down through the years and has since warmed the hearts of all who have heard it. The last surviving workman — a water boy on the job — died nearly a century ago. He was the last to know the location of the Book and the reason behind it all.

The mill still stands on the bank of the Canasawacta Creek, on the west side of the city. It has never been known to be idle. For many years farmers from the hills brought their grain there and took home flour, meal, and oatmeal, for their stock and themselves.

The old mill still houses piles of bran sacks filled with many kinds of feed. It may not be ground there, but just as our ancestors picked up their grain, loading onto the old buckboard from the high platform, we can back our trucks in and pick up our grain supplies.

THE ORIGIN OF "WHITE STORE"

Most of the villages and hamlets were called by the first settler's surname as a matter of course, or named in fond remembrance of the place they had last called home. A few vicinities in Chenango County are still carrying the Indian titles given them long before the white man came.

But the case of a little community nestled in the hills a few miles from Norwich is different.

In the fall of 1802, David Shippey and his young wife came from the East. It was shortly after the Revolutionary War. As they traveled westward on a wagon route, leaving Albany, they came to a beautiful valley. The rolling hills were ablaze with autumn splendor. The bright reds, greens, yellows and orange sparkled in the midday sunshine.

The Shippeys stopped the oxen and just drank in the glorious colors before them. Never before had they seen such an array of Nature's beauty.

As they sat in the cart holding hands, an overwhelming desire struck David — "It has been a long journey from that last inn and according to my directions it is over a day's ride to the next one. This is such a beautiful valley, a place for the weary traveler should be right here."

In 1803 David Shippey was making his dreams come true. All winter they had cut trees and hewn lumber to build this dream.

Other travelers passed along the road and Mr. and Mrs. Shippey would invite them into their humble cabin to rest and enjoy a hot meal.

The young couple had made many friends before David officially opened his trading post.

As their popularity grew, the trading post became a tavern, a store, a news source and a community gathering place. In fact it was a life line to Albany, the Hudson River and New York.

The settlers for miles around brought in their furs and wool from their sheep and other things like maple sugar, wild honey and brilliant pheasant plumes. Things the people in New York City would gladly pay good money for. David had the reputation for always making a fair and honest trade.

David Shippey made regular trips to Albany trading the furs and other materials for things that came up the Hudson from New York City. At that time the industrial trade began to be putting out many new inventions and gimmicks to please customers.

When whiskey was three cents a glass and the underground slaves were passing through to Canada, Shippey made his regular trip. When he returned he brought back some white lead, the first ever seen in the new territory. He mixed it with oil and painted the outside of his store.

It was such a bright white, it was almost luminous and the building could be seen by a traveler long before he arrived. On a moonlight night it was like a beacon in the wilderness.

Directions given travelers from points East to Chenango County began to include, "Just beyond the Catskill Turnpike, you'll come to a white store. You can't miss it."

Within a few years after Shippey had built his trading post, a large number of other families had fallen in love with the valley and rolled up cabins.

In fact one day they all gathered at the "White Store" with the profound purpose of building a large church.

In 1820 the church, built on a knoll overlooking the quiet little valley, was finished. It has always been called the White Store Church.

THAR'S COAL IN THEM THAR HILLS

If someone found a vein of gold in the hills of your county, the area would soon be covered with men and shovels. Saloons and dance halls would spring up, as well as trading posts and shacks. That is if it was in the early 1800's!

Yet, back in the days just after the Civil War, coal was discovered in Chenango County, and was gathered two bags at a time. It was just enough to run a little blacksmith shop for a week, and no one in that day could track the discoverer to the vein from which he secretly gathered the fuel. Nor is the secret known today, more than a hundred years later.

The story has been told in other blacksmith shops, until it has become a legend — an unsolved mystery — that will forever plague historians, because it is true and yet so unexplainable.

It was back before the days of the Chenango Canal. Old timers tell us that in those days the blacksmith shops used homemade charcoal to heat their forge fires, charcoal made in a "kiln" in the yard of the shop. It was available as a principal product sold in "charcoal yards" around the community. Householders in that day used wood for home use, but where intense heat was needed, such as that necessary to bend iron, charcoal was an important item.

Down on the site of the present Chenango County Fairgrounds in Norwich stood a little blacksmith shop. Research indicates that the owner, an Englishman, was named Casper Wadsworth and worked alone. A survey of the Wadsworths now living in the area reveals no Casper Wadsworth in any generation, nor is there a blacksmith shop by that name recalled.

Casper was a lone man, but an expert worker in iron. He was a man of the outdoors and took long walks in the evening and on Sundays. Although an expert craftsman and a much needed man in the community he had no friends nor family.

He had a constant fear of marauders and slept on a straw tick in one corner of the shop.

Casper Wadsworth was a devout Christian and although never seen inside of a church he was trusted by his customers. His word on any topic was accepted. He had often been invited to hold public office but instead chose the life of a lonely blacksmith.

It was said that Casper Wadsworth had one good friend who visited him every Sunday.

Back in those days it was customary for the sheriff to allow the more trusted prisoners in his jail to have access to freedom on Sundays. Perhaps Wadsworth's friend was one of these.

At daylight every Sunday, in fair weather and foul, he would show up at the blacksmith shop and go inside. It was known that the two men would breakfast together in the shop. In about an hour they would be seen emerging from the shop, each carrying a gunnysack.

The old blacksmith would carefully snap the padlock on the shop door and then the two men would head for the wooded hill to the east.

Sometime during the afternoon the two men would return, each carrying a bag of what looked like coal on his shoulder. That coal was to become the fire material for the forge, and lasted a whole week.

It has been said that although the men were followed often, they managed to lose their pursuers. No one was ever known to keep track of them, nor to find the source of the black gold.

One Sunday the faithful companion of Casper Wadsworth failed to appear. The police could give no clue as to his disappearance and he was never seen around the village again.

Casper Wadsworth continued his weekly trip to the source of his black gold that once lay somewhere in those hills to the east.

Scarcely a hunter goes among those hills in the autumn without hoping to run across the secret of the long-forgotten blacksmith, who held forth on the site of the fairgrounds, and discovered an element that might have brought riches to the community. The secret still exists somewhere out there in those silent reaches of trees.

BEAUTIFUL WHITE SQUAW

Christmas was near back in 1793 and as Joshua Leland urged his ox team through the mud of lower Madison County, he wondered whether he and his family would reach Hamilton in time to spend Christmas with his friends, the Morris brothers, who had come on before.

Joshua Leland had his family of five children and his beautiful wife, Waistill, in that oxcart that jostled over the muddy ruts, now and then becoming mired. Joshua was 50 and his wife a number of years his junior, and as the oxen trudged along they wondered what the future had in store for them. They had come from Sherburne, Mass., but Leland had been in this wild country once before, having come with the Morris boys a few years before. The land they had actually staked out for their future home was near the land owned by their friends, the Morris's.

As the creaking oxcart reached a place a few miles south of the present hamlet of Pine Woods, at the junction of Routes 26 and 46, the cart was up to its hubs in heavy mud. Worse still, it was beginning to freeze and the weary oxen could go no further. When they finally stopped from sheer exhaustion, Joshua and the oldest boy managed to get them loose from the cart and take them to higher ground. But all knew that their travelling would end there.

Knowing vaguely where he had left the Morris boys on his last trip, Joshua set out on foot, across the country toward the settlement of what was then known as "Slab City". He finally arrived at his friend's home and together they made the five mile trip back to where the cart was stuck in the mud. Lean-to protection was hastily provided and the whole party spent the night near a blazing fire of pine boughs.

It was while sitting around the fire that the men decided that it would be much easier and more practical to build their cabin on that spot, instead of trying to get the oxcart out of the mud. So in the morning the sound of axes rang through the forest, and by night the framework of a cabin stood on a hummock a few feet from the encumbered cart.

103

When spring came Joshua Leland began to clear a farm. The beauty of his wife, Waistill, began to be noticed, even by the Indians, who almost worshipped her as a goddess. Indian hunters would leave choice game on the doorstep and Indian mothers brought their sick children to her, believing that she had power to cure them. She became known as the "Beautiful White Squaw," and was virtually a queen. In writing about Waistill Greenwood, which was her maiden name, historians refer to her as the most beautiful woman ever to cross the Chenango River.

Joshua Leland's living was made by making "black salts" or potash, a substance made by burning timber and then slaking the ash. There was no sale for it locally, and the product had to be hauled to Albany by oxcart, packed into barrels. One day Joshua started out and never returned. The brakes on his cart failed while going down a long hill, the barrels struck him in the head, killing him instantly. He is considered to be the first traffic fatality in Madison County.

His body was brought back home and buried near the cabin. The area Indians kept vigil over the grave for several days. This was in June 1810, but the beauteous Waistill managed to keep her family together. She turned the log cabin into an inn, where travelers stopped for cold mutton and a warm drink. Her Indian friends watched over her and the children and no harm befell the "Beautiful White Squaw" or her family.

The Leland family prospered and cleared more land.

A pretty little lake, named for the Lelands, shimmers in the sunshine. Another house stands on the site of the old cabin, a house of many years standing, said to have been built to replace the cabin by a later generation.

A flickering traffic light blinks on the highway in front of the old house, directly over the spot where the oxcart foundered nearly 200 years ago, and where "The most beautiful woman ever to cross the Chenango River" made her appearance in local history.

LADY OF THE FOUNTAIN

It was on a hot Saturday afternoon, some 75 or 80 years ago, when a crowd gathered in the center of Main Street in the village of Norwich, to watch a commotion of those days — a horse down in the road. In the middle of the unpaved street lay one of a team of horses, with the remaining animal standing beside him, probably wondering what had happened to his partner.

Usually, in those days, when a horse fell down, someone would sit on the animal's head to prevent him from getting tangled in the harness, if he tried to get up, which a "down horse" usually did.

A little Negro boy, knowing the rule, ran from the park where he had been playing in the cool shade and promptly sat on the horse's head. But this time it was not necessary. The horse was dead.

The villagers were quite excited over the fate of the horse, a big husky draft animal. It was soon learned that the team had just been driven hard for a considerable distance and it became evident from a veterinarian that it had died of fatigue and thirst. The incident caused a considerable stir in the village. A horse had died of thirst in a town where there was no lack of drinking water. The water was available to humans and dogs, but it could not be reached by a thirsty horse. It seemed that no one thought about a horse being thirsty.

The "stir" that seemed to startle the village did not die down with the passing of time. Instead it became more evident. Several stores on the main street put out tubs, filled with water, for the comfort of thirsty horses. The "Ladies Village Improvement Society", a group of local benevolent women got an idea. Why not start a project to place a public horse and dog drinking fountain in the middle of the main street? The proposal caught the interest of the village people and a fund was started immediately with several good sized contributions by local families. Band concerts, ice cream socials, strawberry festivals and other affairs were held, which helped in the project started by the ladies.

The fountain was finally ordered and was later dedicated with many civic and religious groups taking part, and for several years the cool water slaked the thirst of many animals. It was placed in front of the courthouse, in the center of the street, between the two parks.

The base of the fountain was round and about 12 inches high. Arising from the center was the lovely form of a woman holding a greek vase, from which the water flowed into the base. The "lady of the fountain" faced north to welcome all newcomers to the town.

No one today seems to know how many years the beautiful lady stood guard over the elixir of life, nor can it be estimated how many thirsty animals drew life-giving water from its stone interior. Many old timers of today can remember seeing the fountain in use, but dates seem to be forgotten.

When the first horseless carriages began to roll along the streets of the city, and some drivers weren't used to their machines, the fountain kept getting in the way. Horses were becoming less and less predominant, and the fountain ceased to be needed any more. The new gasoline cars and trucks did not need drinks of water in order to work.

The old fountain was moved. Men and women and children watched its removal, not knowing that what they saw was soon to pose another mystery in Chenango County. A few years after the fountain was taken away, the question arose, "Where was it taken?"

Where did it go? What became of the pretty lady who had graced the center of Broad Street so many years? Today, no one knows.

It is recorded that it was hauled away by a six-horse team, hitched to a low-slung stone wagon, but nothing is said of where it was taken. Was it dumped into a pile of other rubble and covered with dirt? Was it broken into bits and may now be spread on some dumping ground? A thousand people would like to know.

"We called her 'beautiful Jane'," one woman told this writer. "Folks have searched all over the community, but no sign of her has ever been found. Most of those folks who lived at that time are gone with her."

"Beautiful Jane" may never be found again. How such a large statue could vanish so completely still bothers the oldsters of today who were the youngsters of yesterday. All that is left are pictures, although many have vivid recollections of the lady of the fountain.

"It seems like only yesterday," one elderly resident said. "I don't know how we happened to let such a beautiful piece of art get away from us. Why, man, it was one of the most outstanding things in the history of Norwich!"

But beautiful Jane is gone! Perhaps she lies, as many think, under piles of rubble in some newly developed part of the city. Perhaps she was duly buried by some sentimental citizens of yesterday. But where?

That will probably never be known now. All we have are pictures and memories that are still held by those who remember her, and who thought at that time that memories would never be needed.

THE GHOST OF DELAWARE COUNTY

The ghost of Delaware County, East of Chenango, was laid to rest many years ago. The once haunted house, past which children ran in terrified excitement, is now gone and the scene overgrown with brush and wild berries. Even the cemetery where ghostly horses vanished is now a dark and impenetrable forest, silent and fearsome, dotted with the gravestones of those who lived and witnessed the scene. The scene that was even then the beginning of a legend.

But let us go back to the beginning. According to the old timers of the community (and one of them accompanied this writer over the forbidden terrain), there were plenty of grounds for the story that had thrilled the natives around local firesides for over a century.

The story goes back to the year 1811. William McCrea was a highly respected man and a relative of the famous Jane McCrea, whose fate after being accused of being a witch, was a thrill of horror throughout the colonies in 1777. William McCrea came from Sarotoga and settled near what is now Masonville, in Delaware County, just over the southeastern line of Chenango County. McCrea built a mansion-like house and became a leader in the community. In 1829 he was elected a member of the Legislature. Soon after that he died, leaving his wife to live in the big house and to operate the farm.

Mrs. McCrea hired a man by the name of Pangborn, an odd sort of character, and his wife to assist her on the farm. Mrs. Pangborn was an exceptionally beautiful woman, and if spoken to by another man, her husband would flare into a jealous rage. Apparently there was no cause for these outbreaks, as Mrs. Pangborn's character was above reproach and she had the respect of her mistress and the entire village.

One day Mr. and Mrs. Pangborn were putting a load of oat sheaves into the barn when suddenly the horses bolted and came galloping toward the house, the remains of the farm wagon clattering behind them. The maddened animals did not stop as they came very close to the door, but made a quick turn and tore across the road to the cemetery, and according to the legend, were never seen again. In a few minutes Pangborn came to the house, washed his hands and told Mrs. McCrea that his wife was killed by the runaway team. Mrs. McCrea ran to the barn and found the attractive wife bleeding from wounds about her head, but she was too late to save her.

An informal inquest was held and Mrs. Pangborn was buried in the little cemetery across the road. A few days later an ironwood flail, an implement used in that day to thresh out grain, was found in the weeds behind the barn. There was blood encrusted on it and strands of auburn hair, unmistakingly belonging to the lovely lady, just buried.

The body was exhumed and examined. It was found that she had been struck several times on the head with the flail. It was also established that she was not near the horses when she was struck and killed, and the team was probably struck and startled by the flying flail.

Pangborn was immediately arrested and tried. Strangely enough, he was acquitted. He then left the community to go west, where he met and married another beautiful woman. Soon after this marriage, his wife was found dead under circumstances similar to his first wife's demise. This time he did not escape, but was caught and lynched by an infuriated mob of neighbors.

Mrs. McCrea passed away at a ripe old age, and then things began to happen around the old homestead. Eerie lights began to flicker in the vacant house, and on the anniversary of the murder a pair of fiery, dashing horses would race up to the door at midnight and turn and disappear into the cemetery across the road. The old house, avoided by everyone in the neighborhood, finally crumbled into ruins.

Old timers said that ghostly screams continued to come from the barn at intervals, but finally ceased after Pangborn was hanged.

Fletcher Shear was 76 at the time he accompanied me on this trip to the old McCrea farm to inspect the ground upon which the ghostly drama was enacted. He told me many things that surrounded the community's only ghost story. Among them was a prophecy that had been made almost a century before. This prediction warned all people that anyone who dared to tamper with the legend of "The Ghost of Delaware County" would meet a violent end. The story was to remain a legend and get no further.

As I shook hands with my aging guide and thanked him for his assistance, I went back to the office. Upon examining the notes I had taken, I wondered if modern day thinkers could possibly believe such a story. Where could those fiery steeds that Fletcher Shear told about have come from? Certainly no good could come from repeating such a story. The notes were torn from my notebook and filed away in the desk.

But the most unusual part of the story was yet to come, something that made me search out the notes several years later.

A newspaper lay on the desk. In it was a short item that an elderly hermit, over 80 years old, had burned to death in his cabin the night before.

The old hermit was Fletcher Shear!

THE VILLAGE IN THREE TOWNSHIPS

When John Barker, in 1791, pushed his raft up the Chenango River from Binghamton, finally stopping at the mouth of the Tioughnioga and settled, he did not know that he was about to start one of the most unusually located villages in the country — the hamlet of Chenango Forks.

With the coming of Barker and his family to the east bank of the winding Tioughnioga, others began to stop at this fruitful place where the two rivers joined. Subsequent settlers built on both sides of the Barker land and soon the thriving settlement became situated in two counties, Chenango and Broome. Further expansion pushed it into three townships.

So today the hamlet, which stretches along the road for more than a mile, although it has only a few hundred population, is located in the towns of Barker (named for the first settler), Chenango Forks and Greene. This fact, along with its occupancy of territory belonging to two counties, makes considerable bookkeeping for two county clerks and three town clerks.

When the present DL&W Railroad was built, then known as the Utica, Chenango & Susquehanna Valley Railroad, it had its southern terminus at Chenango Forks, with a station at each end of the long village.

At one time the village also had another railroad, the Syracuse, Binghamton & New York, and this had another station in the town, making three railroad stations. The latter road carried loads to nearby Binghamton, but both were finally taken over by the DL&W, now called the Erie-Lackawanna.

Chenango Forks, notwithstanding its railroad facilities and excellent location, never seemed to bother about growing up. It is still the longest small village in the state and many of its present citizens were "born and brought up" within its environs.

A large and beautiful school stands up the road from the center of town. A former hotel, now an apartment house, stands stark and prominent on its main street, a reminder of the old railroad and canal days. The same churches provide for the spiritual needs of the populace that sheltered it many years ago.

Several stores stand along the street, a few of them making a commendable effort to modernize, but with these places of business there are several empty buildings.

Why the village has not grown is not known even by those who have always lived there. It has an excellent location in the midst of fine dairy country. One elderly resident had an opinion.

"We are only a few miles from Greene, which is a fine village, and to the south, less than 15 miles, is Binghamton. Maybe folks don't like the quiet life we live here at the Forks. For me, I was born here and will live here until they cart me up to the cemetery yonder. I love the place."

That may be the answer.

THE BIG BLAST

It was a sharp November night in 1902.

A few hours before the streets of Norwich were filled with marching and milling people. An impromptu parade had taken place, headed by a fife and drum corps and even youngsters with washtubs and tin pans. It seemed that everyone in Norwich, then a large village, was out dancing and prancing in the street.

The activity was the enthusiam of election eve. The populace marched in honor of the hoped-for election of Benjamin B. Odell, Jr., on the following day. The Republicans had outdone themselves and his election was certain.

Anticipating the war-dance and parade a group of practical jokers devised a plan which was kept very quiet until the marchers became tired and left the streets. One by one the windows became dark, and one by one the last men left the saloons for home.

In front of the great courthouse on the village square stood an old Civil War cannon. It had stood there a long time, so long in fact that no one noticed it any more. Whether the work of disgruntled Democrats or whether it just happened, no one knows. But between one and two o'clock in the morning a terrific blast let loose as the old cannon roared out into the night. Never before had such noise been heard. Store windows for several blocks were shattered and many people were thrown from their beds.

Fear gripped the village as men ran out into the streets, some still in their nightshirts. Firemen answered the call and soon the streets were filled again with milling people, gazing at the broken glass and wondering what had happened. All was chaos.

Then it was discovered that the old cannon had been aimed down and a large hole had been blown in the ground.

It was daylight before the streets were empty again. Even those who ran saloons opened them to accommodate the watchers and to replenish the free lunch counters.

113

The next morning the whole village talked. How did the cannon get loaded? Many thought that an old charge had been left in the cannon. The more wise shook their heads. It became more mysterious when the late Harry Saunders came around with his horse and wagon and said he had been engaged to replace the broken windows. He stoutly refused to tell who had hired him. It was several weeks before the damage had been repaired. It was years before the merchants could forgive and forget.

That was 68 years ago, and the mystery had remained a mystery almost all of those years!

Authorities questioned many boys and young men, especially the known local jokesters, some of them young business men of that era. Each steadfastly denied he had lighted the fuse. All seemed innocent.

At the time of the blast no one saw two young men scooting up a back street as fast as their legs could carry them. The boy who had a hand in touching the fuse became a worthy citizen of the city. He managed to keep his secret from his parents and friends for 56 years. It would have been forever if this writer hadn't suspected him after he related several jokes he had played in his youth.

Arthur Dibble, still hale and hearty, sat in his yard with me. With a little urging, he told the story.

It seems that he was a young man at the time and unbeknown to anyone a group of jokesters had loaded the cannon with nearly ten pounds of powder and had wadded it tightly with paper. Art and his friend, Shorty Prime, were told of the loaded cannon. Loving a joke themselves, they agreed to touch off the big gun. Straws were drawn and Prime was to light the fuse. From a lookout Dibble was to give the signal.

They waited until the streets were deserted and young Dibble struck a match. It was the signal. By the time the gun went off the two boys were nearly a mile away. That was pretty decent running in any man's language! It was a good thing too, considering the damage done.

Old timers still recall that hectic night. Had the boys been caught at the time they might well have been boiled in oil on the courthouse lawn. The years mellowed the escapade.

The cannon was deactivated after the firing. Later it was picked up in a scrap drive to help fight World War I. All has been forgiven now.

Asked the identity of the real leaders in the escapade, Art shook his head.

"They are all gone now," he said. "Let them rest in peace. Shorty and I fired the thing, that's all that matters now."

And I guess he was right.

POOR MAN'S HEAVEN

PORK AND BEANS, ALL YOU CAN EAT, FIVE CENTS!

FRESH HOMEMADE PIE, FIVE CENTS!

A PLATEFUL OF POTATO SALAD, OR A LARGE BOWL OF CLAM CHOWDER — STILL FIVE CENTS!

One living in Norwich wouldn't have to be very old to remember "Red" Mathewson's "Poor Man's Heaven."

High school students, railroad men, policemen, office workers and even tramps, found their way to Red's "Heaven" on North Broad Street, back in 1934, and according to Red's own statement, "No one ever left hungry, whether he had money or not."

Noah C. Mathewson, known in Norwich all of his life as "Red", was a railroad man. Red had lunched all up and down the railroad line and by 1934 had become tired of, as he says, getting gyped and paying twice the value of good food and getting an inferior grade. Red liked to eat. His large frame and jovial face attested to that. But it irked him to spend his good money for food that didn't seem to satisfy him.

Red began to mull the situation over in his mind. Why not start a different kind of restaurant, a place where the poor man could come and eat and still get the same grade of food that the rich man enjoyed. He began to figure. He stayed up late at night, after working all day, making his plans. He found famous pie recipes by writing to distinguished chefs. He wrote to a man on the coast of Maine and received the best clam chowder recipe in the world. He arranged with a butcher to provide grade A beef for hamburg. Soon he had all his plans on paper.

Then he rented the store on the corner of Henry and North Broad streets in the city. A long table was built and chairs provided. In the back a kitchen was built, and when Red had arranged for his first order of provisions he inserted a double page ad in the daily newspaper.

Soon, from a modest order of ten pounds of hamburg from the butcher, the order rose to 50 pounds a day and then to 100 pounds. From five pies a day, the order jumped to 50, then a hundred.

Mrs. Pat Barber was working full time, baking pies for "Poor Man's Heaven." On big days, Red would sell 100 pounds of ground beef, made into the traditional hamburgers, in as short a time as an hour and a half. Dozens of old-fashioned shortcakes disappeared in a hurry during the strawberry season.

Of his clam chowder Red was justly proud. On chowder days he used to make as much as 20 gallons, and folks who liked chowder, but didn't care for the atmosphere of Red's "heaven" (which catered mostly to men) took it home in cardboard containers. A special day for chowder was Friday.

Searching around the countryside Red made contacts with farmers and others for fresh genuine buttermilk, "with the butter still floating around in it," and of this he sold 150 gallons every few days — ice cold and delicious. Men and boys dropped in every day and sometimes several times a day, for a shot of Red's buttermilk. A big glass cost a nickle, and if you needed a second one, it was free.

In those days, when business boomed in "Poor Man's Heaven" Red organized a softball team and had a large car to cart the team to the games. An iron-handed manager, he always stipulated he would take the boys to the game in the car, but if they lost they would have to walk home. This included games played in Oxford, Sidney, Sherburne or anywhere else. Needless to say most of the games were won by Red's team.

By and by trouble began to knock at the door of "Heaven." Red, a stickler for law and order, had begun to write his views of local affairs and some of the less known political "secrets" on the large show windows of his Heaven. This greatly increased his homey atmosphere in the restaurant, but some of the city fathers were distressed. He was warned, but believing in freedom of the press, the warnings were unheeded.

117

As the "Poor Man's Heaven" was situated next door to the local bus station, strangers changing buses were kept amused as they waited for their next bus. Every morning a crowd would gather in front to read the latest local gossip. Some were pleased but the local dignitaries were not impressed. They never knew who would be next. Finally Red was taken down to see the Police Chief. Red was accused of committing a "breach of the peace." The result of the trial, where Red handled his own case, adorned in a new suit, a bright yellow shirt and a plug hat, is local history. "Poor Man's Heaven" was doomed. The doors closed and some of the other restaurants in town took heart and began to dust off their counters.

Red got a job working for the railroad again. He sat in the tower on East Main Street and watched for trains to appear out of the horizon, and raised and lowered the gates for the Lackawanna.

Retired now, the man who was born on the north shores of Chenango Lake, claiming to be a member of the oldest tribe in Chenango County, is getting ready to pick up where he left off several years ago.

"And," said Red to this reporter, as he put on his hat and lit a fresh cigar, "My next 'Heaven' will have angels in it!"

WHO WAS BOBBY?

Who was "Bobby"?

Who was the little boy who died 30 years ago and lies buried in a lonely grave in a rural cemetery in Oneida County — and in the potter's field of the little cemetery?

And who came, after several years, and placed a clean white stone, upon which was chiseled the child's first name and the date of his death — "Bobby, March 23, 1940"?

Was it his mother, who may have been separated from him at the time of his death, who came to pay her belated respects to her child?

The answers to these questions may be contained in a record book locked in the sexton's desk, but churchyard sextons do not tell wandering newspapermen the secrets of those who lie buried in the potter's field. It may be well that he doesn't. Those who lie there in silent anonymity might not wish to have their unfortunate stories spread upon pages for all to see.

Bobby's name, as far as we have been able to determine is unknown. After talking with the sexton, I did learn that Bobby was a frail child and when he was about two years old his mother placed him in a foster home and went away. Perhaps she hoped that someday she might be able to provide a home and a mother's love for her boy, but like many other hopes, this was denied her.

When Bobby was eight years old, we learned, he was taken with an incurable malady against which he had no resistance. After many months of paralyzed suffering, peace came to Bobby, alone and away from the mother who loved him.

Here the sexton stopped in his story. He looked over toward the little white stone in the field.

"Bobby apparently had no friends or any money," he said. "We buried him over there with public funds. Later, money came from somewhere and paid for the burial costs. We never learned from where."

The grave was unvisited for a long time, and then one morning when the sexton came to work, there was a lovely white stone sitting on Bobby's grave, all inscribed with the proper words. Apparently some one had brought it during the night and put it exactly where the lonely child sleeps in potter's field.

That is the story. Behind it may lie another story that the world will never know. The mother's grief at learning the fate of her child, the pangs that must grip her heart when she thinks of him lying there among the other unfortunates in potter's field. It is like a dark page in her life. Time may heal it or good fortune may some day allow her to give him a better resting place, but perhaps she too, has gone and they are at last together.

After this story was published in 1967, I received a letter from a family in Chenango County who had read the story. They had small children and decided to adopt Bobby's grave. They visited it regularly putting flowers on it and keeping it trimmed. Bobby is no longer alone, he has brothers and sisters and parents who love him as if he were their own.

Meanwhile, Bobby lies in the only marked grave in the potter's field in a country cemetery near Waterville. Above him the birds sing just as sweetly as they do over where the big monuments are. On his little grave the leaves of autumn fall just as gently, and the sunbeams play just as prettily as they do on the others further up the path.

PHARSALIA IS BORN

It was in the early summer of 1791 that several pair of oxen, hauling carts loaded with household goods plodded over the rough country between Oxford and what is now known as the Town of Pitcher. Oxford was then a mere settlement and when the carts stopped there on their way from Schenectady, it was found that there was little food and supplies available, so it was decided to move on.

As the crude caravan moved up through what is now McDonough, the four men wondered what was before them. They had blazed the trail from the tiny settlement of Oxford, in case they needed to return for such meagre supplies as the people could afford.

Finally, two weeks later, the caravan stopped in more open country. One of the men had downed a deer and there was food for all that night. After a good night's sleep under the pine boughs the men held a conference. "Why go any further?"

Here was food, some clear land and a stream which abounded with fish, probably the Otselic River.

The four families began to build cabins and soon smoke was curling up from a new settlement, later to become the hamlet of Pharsalia. The first winter, 1791-92 was a tough one and the pioneers were not prepared, but they managed to survive the cold and the deep snow. With the coming of spring, they learned that John Lincklaen, an agent for the Holland Land Co., had acquired all of the land for a big development. The company had planned to bring colonists here from the east and deeds to the land occupied by the settlers had already been transferred.

The little company of settlers was headed by Ebenezer Fox, Jacob Noteman, Abram Dorn and John VanAuger. A little later the family of Silas Burgess, settled a few miles to the south of them.

John Lincklaen became a friend of the settlers. He was trusted and admired for his skill as a civil engineer as well

121

as his availability in time of need. Somehow he managed to let the families retain the land they had worked so hard clearing and planting. There are many stories of the kindness of this man, who had more to do with the opening up of the tract than any other. A small township in the northwest corner of Chenango County bears his name with honor.

One day an Indian stopped at the settlement of Pharsalia and told of men working in the woods many miles to the north, cutting down trees. He told of the strength of the axmen, and of the ox teams at work hauling logs and brush. He had no idea what it was all about, but the white man was surely tearing up the forest.

This caused considerable conversation among the villagers. What could this mean? Within weeks the sound of falling trees could be heard in the distance, later the sound of axes were audible. Then came speculation on the character of the invaders. What were they doing?

One morning the engineer in charge of the operation rode into town ahead of the axmen. He was a cordial fellow and told the settlers that within a week his men would have completed chopping a road between their settlement of Pharsalia and Cazenovia, then the largest village within hundreds of miles.

In Cazenovia there was a trading post, a general store, a blacksmith shop and even medicines. The trip could be made on horseback in about a day. The engineer painted the picture of years to come when a stage would run over the new road.

The folks of Pharsalia were jubilant. That night the workmen and teamsters were invited to be guests of the people at a dinner and merrymaking time. The women had a whole day to prepare for the feast and in late afternoon a dozen scrubbed and sunburned husky men arrived for supper, which was served under the trees in the settlement.

It was the most enthusiastic event ever held in the community, so enthusiastic that the two main axmen, John Wilson and James Smith were destined to live in the vicinity. They were both from New Jersey, husky and handsome, probably hired by the road clearing company for their strength and prowess with an ax. Smith decided to stay right then and settled near DeRuyter.

The new road proved a godsend to the people and to the community. Over it came craftsmen and others looking for a new place in which to settle and make a living.

Mr. Fox opened a cooper shop, and in 1794 John Lincklaen persuaded John Wilson to come back and build a mill nearby for Lincklaen, using power from the Otselic Creek. Later Lincklaen sent a carpenter to build a frame house, the first in town.

Pharsalia didn't prosper, although all around it villages began to grow. In a few years the stages began to run and although no longer isolated, Pharsalia was not destined to show much growth. Many of the early farms are now embraced in the thousands of acres of state land in that section of the county.

When John Wilson came to erect the mill he never missed Sunday religious services. One Sunday he met Jonas Hinman, one of the leaders of the little church group. John was invited to visit the Hinmans and have dinner. He was introduced to Polly, the daughter. John had seen the demure young lady at the meeting house, but now he was smitten.

The next time Lincklaen came, Wilson begged permission to operate the mill for him. The request was granted. In May, 1799, John and Polly were married in the first wedding ceremony to take place in the town.

The old road, hewn out of the forest by strong woodsmen, is still in existence, and winds its way up through the town of Otselic to its destination in Cazenovia.

THE SILENT IMPOSTER

"Dr. Jekyll and Mr. Hyde" was a figment of the imagination of Robert Louis Stevenson, but "Dr. Livingston and Mr. Hewitt" was the brain child of no writer, for the "Great Dr. Livingston" lived and practiced both hoax and chicanery in Chenango County just about the time "Dr. Jekyll" was having his fling in the imagination of Stevenson.

The story of Dr. Livingston is a complex story. Between the lines one can see the battle between good and evil, kindness and cruelty, love and despair. It is a story of a gigantic, yet fearful hoax carried on for 50 years and disclosed only on the deathbed of the man who finally grew tired of living a masked life.

The story is laid in the tiny hamlet of Bennettsville in the southeastern part of Chenango County back about 1847. At that time there stood on the Esopus Turnpike a large inn called the "Caravansary," overlooking a beautiful valley. On all sides raised the Chenango hills, like the humps on the backs of huge camels, stretching for miles and disappearing into the blue haze in the distance.

Such was the sight that greeted the occupants of an elegant carriage that drew up to the door of the inn one spring day. Two men alighted and waved to the coachman to put the horses in the stable. One man, somewhat older than the other, introduced his companion as, "The Great Dr. Livingston," a deaf mute, but insisted that he was a very learned doctor. Dr. Livingston was young, dashing and handsome. And, not the least, interested in meeting him was the younger of the inn keeper's daughters, Electa Matteson.

Electa was fair-haired and beautiful and just blossoming into womanhood. She had been educated in the little schoolhouse near the fork in the road, and had never been beyond the chain of hills. Anyone who came from out of that blue haze must have come from a world of wonder to the innocent Electa.

Electa felt sorry for the man who could communicate only with a slate, and this pity soon developed into love as the doctor went about treating the sick of the community. His companion, Mr. May, had returned to the East.

One day a message came which seemed to disconcert Dr. Livingston. On his slate he wrote that he must return immediately to New York City. Electa watched the carriage disappear off into the blue haze, wiped her eyes and went back to her work in the kitchen. The world seemed to have come to an end for the innkeeper's daughter.

Not long after, a rider galloped up to the inn and handed Electa a letter. It was from her lover, directing her to come to New York. She packed her clothes and immediately left on the next stage, thinking Dr. Livingston might be in some kind of trouble and needed her.

Electa was confused, but when the handsome doctor embraced her at the station in New York, she felt relieved and happy. So it was natural that when he proposed marriage she accepted eagerly. The two were married, but the following day the first disconcerting incident occurred.

A young woman approached her in the lobby and upbraided her for being in the hotel with her husband, Lewis Hewitt. Electa was shocked and sought out her husband. Words followed. The doctor admitted that he was married and had not had a divorce. It was also revealed that he was not deaf and dumb, but had affected it to get ahead as a doctor and to induce sympathy. He extracted a promise from the girl to guard his secret forever.

Remarried following the doctor's divorce, "Dr. and Mrs. Livingston" returned to Chenango County where he set up a practice, still using his slate for communication. The little town of Bennettsville came to love the couple and the doctor did a flourishing business. Every so often the good doctor would go to New York to keep up on modern medicine. A daughter was born to the happy couple and all seemed well.

A few days after the doctor departed for New York on one of his business trips, Bennettsville was swept by a plague of diphtheria. Electa and their seven-year-old daughter were the first victims.

They died before the doctor could get back, but he managed to arrive in time for their burial.

Dr. Livingston was distraught. He became a different man.

Then sensing a chance to get rid of the yoke he had carried so long, he started to speak and said the shock had restored his speech.

There were those who were skeptical, being unable to understand how one who had not spoken since childhood, could use such perfect English. Others still had faith in their doctor but in just a few years he passed on to meet his little family.

Several relatives and friends came from New York for his funeral and it was disclosed that he was really Lewis Hewitt and had not studied medicine, but used a few Indian methods with considerable luck.

In Bennettsville Cemetery near Bainbridge is a monument marking the grave of Dr. Livingston or Lewis Hewitt as he was christened in 1822. His death in 1894 revealed a double life that would certainly puzzle one in this day and age.

THE VALLEY'S FIRST NEWSPAPER

Now and then one runs onto a very interesting story in the most humble hamlet. An old timer sitting in front of the general store, an elderly gentleman scything grass in front of his home, or a country doctor who has just driven up to a home where sickness is present — each may say something that could lead to a story that other folks have long forgotten.

This is true of the little hamlet of Sherburne Four-Corners where a metal marker tells that a house still standing by the side of the road was the home of the first newspaper in Chenango County.

Being a one time rural editor it was not diffucult for this writer to imagine the composing stones, the old hand press, the type cases and the office stove. I could see in retrospect as it were, the old sale bills tacked on the walls as samples, the dim oil lamps and the printer in smudged apron seated on a high stool, and selecting type from the cases. He was placing the type in a "stick," a contrivance used in setting each line to exact measurement. Perhaps, like most old-time printers he was smoking an old much-used pipe, filled with cut leaf.

However intriguing the imagined picture may have been, the real story of Abraham Romeyn and his brother Nicholas, the first printers to ride into Chenango County to start a newspaper, was even more interesting.

It was back in 1803 when upstate New York was little more than a wilderness, with a few large settlements scattered around. Abraham Romeyn had been in the newspaper business in Johnstown, one of the larger villages and had been bested by a competitor and forced to give up.

A few days after he had closed his doors, Abraham Romeyn, an alert man, and his brother who was slower but industrious, saddled their horses and started out to find another place where a newspaper would be needed. Sherburne at that time was just a settlement of a few log houses, but

127

further along was what was known as "Sherburne-Four", where there was more activity. No one knows today why Sherburne-Four gave up its claim to being one of the busiest places in Chenango County to what is now the humming village of Sherburne. Now mainly residential, Sherburne-Four is a quiet little hamlet where a few homes attest to the once busy settlement with stores, blacksmith shops, a school and cheese factory.

Abraham and Nicholas rode from the east and stopped at Sherburne. They were disappointed in the smallness of the place, but an old fellow smoking his pipe in front of a blacksmith shop directed them to the busy settlement, four miles further to the west. They headed in that direction, although they were tempted to turn back.

It was late afternoon when they arrived and the travelers were tired and hungry. They found a family who took them in, and the men were fed the finest meal they had eaten in months. The family was equally pleased to hear the news the men brought. They talked of President Thomas Jefferson and Vice President Aaron Burr. News was scarce in upstate New York, and came only from travelers such as the two printers who eagerly feasted on roast beef.

The two decided to set up their newspaper at Sherburne-Four and after about a week they had engaged a shed behind a farmhouse, which later became the newspaper office.

They saddled up and rode through the autumn sunshine back to Johnstown. They were in a happy frame of mind, and as they rode back through the Sherburne village, they waved happily to the old gentleman who was again sitting in front of the blacksmith shop.

By early winter the Romeyn brothers had their printing equipment loaded in an ox-sled and started back to the hamlet of which they had such fond memories.

Their arrival in Sherburne-Four was celebrated by a dinner in the home in which they first stayed. By the time the geese began to fly north the shop was in order and plans were made for the first paper. One day in March the first impression was made. This first paper is still in the possession of the Charles Merrill family of Sherburne-Four.

The paper, called the Western Oracle, is on blue paper of excellent quality.

But the Romeyns could not brook competition. In 1808, the Olive Branch sprang up in Sherburne, and the Romeyns sold their equipment and holdings and the Olive Branch became their successor. The Olive Branch soon became The Volunteer, and in 1816 was purchased by John F. Hubbard and became The Norwich Journal. This was merged with the Oxford Republican, and was published in Norwich under the name of Chenango Union.

The Chenango Union is still published in Norwich by Lewis Phelps, along with his son. The paper is now printed on modern presses in a modern shop and the editor is proud to point out many names on his subscription list, who are descendants of the original readers of the old Western Oracle.

When the Romeyn brothers rode off into the summer twilight, they left many happy memories with the residents of Sherburne-Four, but no one seems to know where they went or if they were ever heard from again. Whether it was heartbreak, or tragedy along the road, will never be known.

"IF ALL THOSE PACK PEDDLERS . . ."

If all the pack peddlers whose bodies are said to be resting under Chenango County farm porches, under barns and old historic houses were lying end to end — well, it would be quite a scary spectacle.

In my years as a writer, I have heard of more than a dozen stories of pack peddlers who came to various old homes on Saturday nights — it was always on a Saturday night — to ask for weekend lodging. It seemed they always came just as the mortgage was due and there was no money in the cigar box under the bed. Pack peddlers were always loaded with money by Saturday night and — well, why go into the story further? Let us just say that the pack peddler didn't trudge up the road Monday morning, or that someone was seen digging under the porch by lantern light Saturday night. Or to make it less fearsome, we could say that the mortgage was paid up in full on Tuesday!

In our earlier days we were often tempted to believe such yarns, and probably did take stock in some of the more probable ones, but what reporter is going to walk up to the door of some of our fine old country homes and ask if the family knew there was a man buried under their porch? I wonder how I would feel if someone asked me that question.

But such yarns still persist. Just recently I was told that under the front porch of a fine old area home lies the remains of a pack peddler who was known to everyone of that day. One night he stopped at the house for lodging and was ushered to a stall in the barn. The next morning he wasn't there, and it was a known fact that horses do not eat pack peddlers. Many years afterward someone told down at the corner pub that somebody else's Uncle Joe remembered that a friend of his grandfather had heard in another saloon across the river that someone was seen digging under the porch by lantern light that very night — yes, sir, that very night! The moon was clouded over and four owls sat on a sycamore tree. And if there ever was a sign of disaster that was it!

130

Five years after this the gas company man in digging up a gas main discovered the bones of a man. In the skull was a gold tooth and it was known that a certain pack peddler who used to frighten the neighborhood had a gold tooth.

We have never learned how many householders started digging under porches after hearing these stories, but we feel that some day a story hunting author may investigate and then procede to write a best seller.

It was many years ago that this writer and a group of boys were walking along the banks of the Owasco River and came upon a wierd spectacle. Hanging from a lower limb of a maple tree on the river bank was the body of — yes, you guessed it — a pack peddler. A note pinned to the man's vest gave the name of the next of kin and directions as to the disposal of the body.

Pack peddlers were part of the scene in the early part of the century and many of them were women, but they knew how to drive a hard bargain.

The author remembers as a boy the thrill of looking into those canvas packs as the peddler displayed them to his folks.

In the pack, which was always neat, were arranged such things as pencils, rolls of elastic, thread, needles, pins, hooks and eyes, snaps, handkerchieves, stockings and other items that a housewife so often needed. When the girls of a family viewed the merchandise they would squeal with delight at the many rolls of colored ribbons, celluloid combs, hairpins and fancy buttons.

The old pack peddler, whether he now rests under a porch or not is a thing of the past. No longer does he trudge the dusty roads or knock on the farm house doors. It may be that he sees danger in this today — danger that didn't exist when he was free to walk the roads as he wished and sleep under a haystack or in a barn stall.

They were welcomed by most families, even those with no money, who enjoyed looking at the contents of a peddler's valise.

The pack peddler of yesterday was the fore-runner of the traveling salesman of today. Although the ancestors may be reposing under porches, their sons and daughters are "big business" today, still using their fast glib talk to persuade the unsuspecting customer that he needs a new roof on his house or a more up-to-date furnace.

Regardless of those molding pack peddlers, Chenango County is rich in folklore. There is hardly a field, patch of forest land or hillside, but which could say much if it could talk.

OSCEOLA

Every village has its unusual characters, and Sherburne was no different from any other village in that respect. Some of the real old timers in Sherburne may still remember stories of Sally Tucker, one of the most unusual persons ever to grace a community with her presence.

Sally Tucker came to Sherburne during the old Chenango Canal days. Legend has it that she and her husband were employed on a canal boat and on the day the canal was closed forever Sally and her husband, Seth Tucker, happened to be on a boat that was tied up in Sherburne. This fact didn't bother the couple. Knowing that the boat would be left at the place it had stopped, they decided to make the canal boat their home. That is how this very unusual person came to Sherburne.

Even though she was uneducated, uninhibited and ignorant of letters, her name will go down in history. For Sally had the trait that all should seek — the faculty of being kind without appearing to try, and enduring long suffering without realizing it.

A few years later, Seth Tucker died, leaving Sally a widow. Dates are a bit scarce in Sally's story, but it is known that shortly after the death of her husband she built or was given, a shack in the glen at the top of Rexford Falls, a few miles east of the village. There the legend had its beginning.

Sally was, as she often boasted, "one half white, one half Negro and the other half Indian." She was especially proud of the "one half Indian" and claimed to be a direct descendant of the Seminole Chief Osceola and took the name Osceola, instead of Sarah, her given name, or her nickname "Sally."

Sally Tucker earned pennies by working in homes around the village. She had a knowledge of herbs and was often called upon to treat villagers with such nostrums as grew in the woods and fields. Osceola was kindly — too kindly for her own good — and although many villagers chose to smile depreciatively at her brand of kindness, she was the one called upon when other measures failed.

133

Osceola had four husbands in her lifetime, losing each when the herbs of the fields failed to save them. She was deeply religious and attended the Episcopal church in the village.

Although Sally had had three husbands before she married Seth, she always claimed she loved Seth Tucker most of all, and when the "yarbs" as she called them, failed to save him, her heart was broken. She never credited herself with knowledge, but termed it, "the work of the Lord." Always ready and willing to give a hand to the ladies of the community, she received little pay and if someone gave a dish of food or an old discarded piece of clothing to her, she was eternally grateful.

Sally spent the last years of her life alone, doing good where she could and ministering to the sick and the lowly, often depriving herself of food so that someone else could eat. During the summer she would pick the wild berries around Sherburne and give them away, to make a family happy with a shortcake or two.

Finally Osceola had to curtail her long walks to the village and it seemed the herbs were losing their power to help her. She grew older and had to start depending on the friends she had served so well most of her life.

It has been said that given the chance of a normal life, she might have been a beautiful woman, a typical Indian princess. But life had dealt cruelly with Sally Tucker. The rough life on the canal boats, the foraging for food and the housework and doctoring had taken its toll.

One night, about midnight, in some forgotten manner, word came to Mr. and Mrs. Redmond Lowe that Sally was very sick in her little hut on top of the ravine.

Kindly neighbors went to see her and decided she should be taken to the Lowe home so she could have better care.

A few days later Sally Tucker, or "Osceola" as she liked to be called, sighed deeply, and her tired soul drifted over into that other valley, where her lost childhood lay.

She was given a decent burial and the whole town of Sherburne mourned the loss of such a friend indeed. Her grave is probably on the Lowe farm on East Hill just outside of Sherburne, but her works and kindness shall ever live on.

A PIANO FACTORY COMES TO NORWICH

If one could be whisked back a century to the Norwich, in Chenango County of the days before the Civil War, he would find a vastly different community than he sees today.

The village, and it was just a village at that time, was cut in half by the winding, slow-moving Chenango Canal, and canal men became a Saturday night scourge, with their brawling.

David Maydole, a young blacksmith, had just begun to operate a factory to make his famous hammers. On the bank of the canal, the Sawyer boys were building a cooperage shop, and two other young men, Morse and Kershaw were starting a sash and blind factory between what is now the VFW Home and Silver Street. The canal came down what is now State Street and west of what is now the Berglas Manufacturing Company.

The present Stone Mill was grinding grain and a machine shop stood behind where the Victory Chain offices are. The stores were of the "general" store type, carrying anything from sugar to buffalo robes. A half dozen blacksmith shops were scattered around, all doing business and all furnishing free entertainment for farmers and others on rainy days.

It was about this time that Edward A. Hayes, an ambitious 26-year-old, with $150 capital and a knowledge of piano making, decided to step out for himself. Hayes had learned about pianos from working for Utley & Smith at Guilford. Hayes had learned that there was a difference between a good piano and an excellent one. His aim was to make the best piano in the world, and in the first year he turned out four and it was hard painstaking work. Then his brother, who had been working with him, decided that it was too slow work with not enough remuneration for the effort spent, and left to find a more stable job.

A man named George H. Lattin approached Hayes saying he had a little money he would like to invest. Hayes took him up on it and they formed a partnership. Then George Rider, a wealthy man in the village, bought a third interest. Not long after, Lattin died and his holdings were purchased by John Slater and the firm was reorganized to become E. A. Hayes & Co.

The firm turned out what they believed to be the best pianos in the world and most of these were purchased by artists all over the world. Later the pianos were named Hayes & Rider pianos and under this name the business flourished.

About 1875 competition began to creep in — competition that Messrs. Hayes and Rider could not brook without lowering the quality of their product. Unscrupulous competition in the form of inferior instruments and lower prices, cut deeply into the business. Buyers bought the cheaper pianos not knowing the difference, until it was too late to return them.

Stockholders began to withdraw from the firm and Hayes and Rider were left alone. Under these odds they continued, steadfastly refusing to make an inferior piano. Consequently they saw their business dwindle until the day when the final piano, still the best in the world, left the factory.

But Hayes & Rider had set a standard that the inferior pianos could not attain, and later their niche was filled by other manufacturers who started to make fine pianos assembly line style, thus keeping up the standard demanded by succeeding generations of artists.

There are still a number of Hayes & Rider pianos in existence, all in fine condition and all showing the superior workmanship put into them by the artisans at the old Hayes & Rider piano factory, which is now a part of the spreading Norwich Pharmacal Company plant on Eaton Ave.

In fact that street was named Piano Street until a few years ago, when it was renamed Eaton Avenue in honor of the Eaton family, who founded the Norwich Pharmacal Company.

Thus was lost a fine business because two Norwich men long ago decided to remain honest, and give the world their very best.

HECTOR ROSS, INDUSTRIALIST

Back in 1837 a young Scotch youth trudged along the turnpike that stretched from Buffalo towards Albany, on foot. Penniless and unacquainted with the customs of America, young Hector Ross was assailed by many thoughts.

In those days there were no relief agencies, no rescue missions where a hungry lad could go for food and no free accommodations. The hot sun burned down on him one day and rain pelted his face the next, but the poorly clad and half starved Scotch boy kept on depending upon such food as he could get along the way, from settlers and Indians.

While Hector Ross is plodding along it might be well to tell of his background. Born in Greenlock, Scotland in 1811, a son of a molder, young Ross dreamed of the wonders of America. Working his way across the sea, he landed in Canada, where he worked for a few days at his father's trade and then set out on foot to Buffalo, where he expected to find work. Young Ross, who was destined much later in life to build the largest manufacturing plant in Sherburne, New York, met his first disappointment in Buffalo and although tired, lonesome and hungry, he set out on foot toward the East with no knowledge of his destination. He needed work and food and needed it badly.

Days later he stumbled into Oneida, then little more than a settlement. He found a single day's work in a knitting mill where one of the hands was absent for the day. It is there that Hector Ross found the work he thought he would like better than molding. Learning there might be work in one of the two mills then in New Berlin, he again set out, only to find that there was no job for him.

Young Ross was allowed to sleep on a pile of sacks in a store that night and the next day the storekeeper told him of a knitting mill further on at Morris. He again set out and at last found work as a hand mule spinner at $18 a month.

Hector Ross liked his new job, found favor with his employer and remained in the employ of the mill for the next

20 years, the last six of which he was mill superintendent. In the meantime he married a girl in the village and had become a respected citizen, active in church and business life of the village.

He was then 45 and wanted a business of his own. Unable to buy into the mill at Morris he went to New Berlin where, with his brother, who had followed him from Scotland, he purchased one of the mills. A few years later he sold his interest to his brother and purchased a large farm.

Hector Ross, who knew all there was to know about a cotton mill, did not make a good farmer. He wanted to get back into his old business. Selling the farm he moved to Sherburne where he invested his savings in the erection of a knitting mill, the building still standing on North Main Street. The subsequent owners, Utica Knitting Co. relocated a few years ago because of competition. The building is now owned by Chesebrough-Ponds, Inc., manufacturing surgical bandages and related items.

It was a great day, that May 6, 1862, when Hector Ross laid the first brick in the new mill. It was also his 51st birthday and that brick signified the beginning of a new and greater Sherburne. A few years later Ross had purchased the interest of the few stockholders who had bought into the business and became the sole owner, the mill entirely paid for.

Hector Ross, besides being a man of exceptional ability and business acumen, was a man who understood his workers. Sound in counsel and generous, he helped many of the people of that day over obstacles. He had the faculty of accomplishing great results with little show of activity, and no one loved the quiet Scot more than those who worked under him.

Along with the mill the thrifty employer established a store where his employees could purchase food and clothing at almost cost, one of the first cooperative stores in the nation. He also erected homes, many of which were later sold to the employees.

Sherburne prospered through Hector Ross' venture. Although his own career following the establishment of the business was short-lived, the village grew through means provided for the workers in the mill for many years after. The modern methods of cloth manufacture and the heavy cost of making over the mill in order to cope with the rising competition, caused the final closing of the building as a knitting mill in 1952.

The largest funeral procession ever held in Sherburne bore the remains of the once-tired and footsore Hector Ross to his grave just 10 years after he had laid the first brick for the new mill. He was only 61 when he died, but he had accomplished enough that his name will always be an institution in Sherburne.

BABES IN THE WOODS

It was a bright autumn afternoon when the two children of Faith and Angus Cole started down the hill to the west of that mysterious body of water known as Meade's Pond. The birds were singing in the trees that lined the hillside and there seemed to be nothing to indicate danger of any kind.

The children were trying to capture polliwogs that darted here and there among the watercress that bordered a spring, now and then squealing with delight when they captured one of the wiggling creatures.

The children were so absorbed in the task that they did not notice the long autumn shadows that had started to come over the hill. growing longer as they spread over the valley. The sharp bark of a fox first told them that the afternoon was waning and it would soon be dark.

The children started in what they thought was the right direction, but when they did not come upon their little cabin they became apprehensive. Darkness was fast enveloping them and they had never experienced nighttime in the forest. Far off to the west the crows were winging their way home, but to children who lived several miles from the place, the homeward flight of the crows meant little. No matter where they looked nothing was familiar. They had started from home about noon, never once thinking about which direction they were taking.

Now they were at a loss to know where they were going. The polliwogs in the spring had attracted their attention for several minutes, but now it was growing darker and the little girl began to whimper.

"I want to go home," she cried. "Mother doesn't know where we are. We must be hundreds of miles away from home. I want my Mother!"

Little Angus put his arm around his sister's waist and tried to comfort her. Together they walked, not knowing they were going the opposite direction from home.

Now they were stumbling over rocks and falling over tree limbs, briars were snagging at their clothing and scratching their bodies. They heard weird sounds coming from the forest and fearfully kept going until they were exhausted. Then the little girl fell over a log, and lay on the ground, calling to her equally frightened brother.

When the children awakened they were in each other's arms, and the bright sun shone in their faces. The birds were singing in the trees and the two were hungry and thirsty. They started down the hillside to the valley where they drank from the clear waters of what later was called Chenango River. Thus refreshed, they walked on, not knowing where the paths in the forest led, but cheered at the rising sun.

On and on the two lost children trudged, growing more and more hungry. A twig snapped in the deer path ahead and an Indian stepped out in front of them.

"You lost?" he asked, as he saw the tear-stained faces of the little ones.

Surprised at the ability of the bronze-cheeked Indian to make himself understood, they ran up to him, grasping his hand.

The Indian told them that he was from Log City, many miles up-stream. He would take them to his cabin if they wished to follow him. He said he had two children of his own and they had plenty of food there.

There was nothing to do but to follow the kindly Indian, who led them over the hills to Log City, which they later learned was the little frontier settlement of Hamilton.

No one in Log City knew the children. They remained with the tall Indian and his squaw, playing with their two youngsters as if they were brothers and sisters.

The Indian and his squaw continued to treat little Angus and his sister as their own. They had warm food and were delighted to wear Indian clothes.

Finally a group of searchers from Oxford learned about two white children up in Log City, who had been found by an Indian hunter over six weeks before. They understood the

141

hunter had been searching for the parents. Perhaps they received this information from a friendly Indian who covered a large territory, hunting and fishing.

Some time later little Angus and his sister met their parents coming toward them in the forest. There were tears of joy and gratitude as the parents and children alike kissed away nearly two months of grief and loneliness.

THE UNHAPPY BLACKSMITH

This story comes from an old copy book and as far as is known no relatives of the kindly Judah Bement remain, although the name appears many times in the history of the Town of Plymouth.

Judah Bement came from Mass. in 1798. Life had been tough for the man in the years following the Revolution. The story is that the Blacksmith had suffered reverses as had all his neighbors. He was a good mechanic and had been singled out to shoe the horses of top army officers during the war. He was once captured by the British, literally stolen away from his forge, and when he refused to perform blacksmithing work for them, he had been thrown bodily out of the shop where he had been told he had to work.

When Judah married his wife, Lydia, he again ran into trouble. He had rivalry for the hand of the young daughter of a shop owner, and had to fight in order to be allowed to live peaceably with his bride, who loved him greatly. Finally one night, after a more or less unpleasant visit from the rival the pair decided to get away from this strife and move to the "West" as all of the land beyond the Hudson was then called.

Judah and Lydia stopped their ox-cart at what is now the village of Plymouth. Only one man had come there before them, a settler named John Miller, who helped the young couple to get a start. Miller helped them roll up a cabin, taking only three days, and then the men built another cabin nearby which was to be the blacksmith shop.

John Miller was a German and had come from a location near Albany but he wasn't particularly fond of the new country and later left to live in what is now Broome County, and later moved to Ohio.

Judah Bement was an ambitious man and soon established a tavern in connection with the blacksmith business. The settlers began to flow "West" in wagon trains and on horseback. Business boomed.

A tavern in those days was not necessarily a drinking place. It was a sort of station by the wayside where travelers

143

put up for the night or stopped for a bite of food. Bement served game, bread and home brewed ale, and settlers stopped at his tavern on the way further west. It became a popular resting place and Bement prospered.

With business booming, the industrious tavern keeper and blacksmith moved to larger quarters. He bought a large farm nearby and built a distillery. He continued to prosper and it was here that his daughter, Mary was born. Although Judah had three other daughters, it was Mary who finally caused the greatest grief that her father had ever experienced.

Mary was never strong. Doctors today might have cured the trouble in her back, but as she lay on her cot, day after day, watching for her father to come home she brought a great deal of sunshine to the family. She was a happy soul and would lie in the window making friends with the birds and squirrels, that would eat from her hands.

Mary grew to young womanhood. Everyone, even the roving Indians, loved her. They brought her gifts and told her stories of the land beyond the sunset. Each night when her father came home, Mary would be waiting for him. Judah then detected a slight lessening of her strength. Within a year she failed fast and on her 19th birthday her sight began to fail, at least that is when she told her father about it.

Mary was known as "The White Angel" to the Indians. She practically became a goddess to them. Her clear features and milky white skin caused them to stand and gaze at her, and one day she failed to see her friends. Although to one looking at her, her eyes looked perfect.

Three years passed. It was March 17, 1839. When her father came home she called to him to please get a drink of cold water from the spring for her. He went back out to the spring and broke the ice to get the water for his daughter. When he returned to the house he found Lydia in tears and the other three daughters sad faced and forlorn. Mary had drifted away to that land beyond the sunset, where her Indian friends had told her there was no sickness or pain.

Mary was buried in the cold earth on the hillside. No one today knows where the grave is located. The family was prostrated. The distillery was shut down and Judah Bement was a broken man. He seemed to have given up, and during the next few years spent many hours beside the grave of his daughter.

The distillery was sold and Judah and Lydia moved to the settlement of Norwich. The other daughters married and lived with their husbands in Pharsalia, Plymouth and McDonough. Lydia and Judah had little to live for now, and a few day before Christmas, 1843, Judah Bement awakened in the land beyond the sunset. Three months later, his wife joined him.

Thus the notes in the copy book ended. The strong man who had defied the British, but whose heart had broken from sorrowful love of his daughter left a mark in the history of Chenango County.

THE SHERBURNE OPERA HOUSE

February 20, 1892 was a cold wintry night. A light snow fell against the store windows in the village of Sherburne, but carriages and open sleighs were drawing up to a large new building on North Main Street, as well dressed men in their plug hats and women with their long gowns entered.

That night marked the opening of the new opera house in Sherburne and one of the biggest crowds in the history of the village gathered to hear the initial bill of the Sherburne Opera House Association, which was to be the New York Philharmonic Orchestra.

In those days the nearest opera house or theater of any size was in Norwich, 12 miles to the south, and a drive on a cold winter's night was often out of the question in those horse and buggy days. Sherburne had long been a town of considerable culture, and as it grew and had larger and better railroad facilities a place of entertainment became a "must."

Real old-timers in the community recall the night of February 20, 1892 as a cold night, but through the driving snow the new opera house was a blaze of light. On this opening night members of the association greeted the first attendants with warm handshakes. By curtain time the 500 seats were filled, while late-comers stood in the back of the auditorium or in the entry hall. Everyone seemed to want to be numbered among the "first nighters".

At the cost of $11,500 the playhouse soon became the talk of the community. Sherburne, being a railroad town, drew some good shows of that day which included some of the stock companies playing "Uncle Tom's Cabin", "East Lynn", "The Old Homestead", with the familiar Si Stebbins and other actors, causing the tears to flow.

Then there were the never-to-be-forgotten minstrels with such well known characters as Lew Dockstader, Hi Henry and others. All of Sherburne turned out to watch the old minstrel parades which preceded these shows, as the fast-playing minstrel band led the group of burnt cork-covered singers and dancers along the street. The familiar plug hats

146

and swinging canes of the minstrel men will long be remembered by lovers of this type of show, as well as the initial command of the interlocutor after the opening chorus: "Gentlemen, be seated!"

The Sherburne Opera House was typical of the "opera house days" of the not-so-distant past. The thickly-carpeted auditorium, the orchestra pit stretching across in front of the stage and the upholstered opera chairs. The late Duane Atkyns once told this writer that as a lad he ushered at the new opera house — the proudest kid in town. His bosom friend, Levant Shepard, whose father was one of the directors, got the position for him. It was a thrill, he said to escort people down the soft carpeted aisle and besides he got to see the shows for nothing.

The first inroads of the movies came with Lyman Howe's Moving Picture Show, which visited theaters all over the country. Older readers will recall the flickering and often outlandish pictures, thrown on a cloth screen by a hand-driven projector. No one realized when Lyman Howe came to town it was the first toll of the death knell for the legitimate theater.

Within a few years the movies had taken over, first the silent pictures which used an orchestra and then the silents with music dubbed into the film. This caused an eruption between the musicians and the theater managers, and marked the beginning of the end of the pit orchestras. The delightfully muffled music of the theater orchestra soon became a thing of the past.

The Sherburne Opera House went through the problems of other opera houses all over the nation, finally losing out to the movies and not too long ago even the movies failed to hold the interest of the crowds. The lights went out forever in the Sherburne Opera House!

But memory is a marvelous thing. Even folks who used to attend those old dramas and minstrel shows of yesterday can see in memory old Si Stebbins, Uncle Tom, Little Eva, Simon Legree and the other greats of an era gone forever, parading before the footlights at Sherburne, but see them only as ghosts — ghosts of the wonderful exciting, extravagant past!

147

TRUMAN ENOS — FAMILY MAN

One of the most colorful characters in early Chenango County history was a crusty old patriarch named Truman Enos. Truly no history can adequately chronicle the events of those days just after 1800 without Truman Enos occupying a conspicuous place in the story. He was known as a man of iron and a figure with which to be reckoned.

When one mentions the name of Truman Enos he is countered with the statement, "Oh, he was the old fellow with a half dozen wives!" That statement is not exactly true. The number of wives has grown with the years. Old Truman Enos had only three wives in his day, although except for the discouragement of his daughter, he might have wedded a fourth, "to see him through," even as the snows of 90 winters crowned his venerable head.

Truman Enos came to Chenango County in 1802 at the age of 23. Tall, muscular, courageous and profane, he soon took a place of leadership in the affairs of the settlement that was later called Norwich. While according to the yardstick of religious leaders of his day he, "did not fulfill the law of God," Truman Enos had so many virtues they literally covered a multitude of sins. Enos is said to have been so wanting in "book larnin'" that he spelled one wife's name three different ways.

Still, the man had plenty of old-fashioned horse sense and bulldog tenacity. Like David Harum, he was one to "Do unto the other fellow what he is going to do unto you — only do it first." Truman Enos got along. His tannery, located where the stone mill now stands in Norwich, was a meeting place for men of the hills and the forests who came to get sage advice from the crusty tanner on the Canasawacta Creek.

Profanity in that day was common. Everybody cussed. Even the clergy had special expressions for special occasions, such as getting kicked by a horse or falling into the creek. This sort of thing was then accepted as common language. The story is told of a hunter in what is now Preston. When all signs failed and he knew he was lost, he dropped to his knees and prayed, "Oh, Lord, You know I am lost. Show me the way home to Betsy and the babies d--n quick." Sure that he had done the proper thing he arose and saw the very signs he was looking for. Such was the crude and simple religion of the pioneer. But it worked.

Truman Enos found religion in almost the same way. Overcome by a sense of guilt while hunting on Sunday, he sought out the only Christian he knew, a Mrs. Snow. There he found peace and never departed from his new found belief in God. His firm dependence on Diety later carried him to leadership in church work and made him one of the prime movers in the building of the present Congregational church in Norwich.

Enos married Lendy Thrall in 1804. She died in 1815. Six months later he married pretty Betsy Campbell, who died two years later from that scourge of the pioneer — tuberculosis. Betsy died in July and the following October he met and married Abby Parmalee while on a visit to Durham, Conn. and brought her back to Norwich. Abby died in 1862.

By this time Enos Truman was getting close to 90. When a census taker asked him if he were married, he snapped "I am nearly 90, have had three wives, but I reckon it will take at least one more to see me through."

He began to court Clarissa Wood, a maiden lady of 61. Clarissa was willing to become his fourth wife, but Enos's daughter, the wife of Dr. Harvey Harris, fought the plan desperately and persuaded her father to change his mind. Enos died a few months later, nearly 92.

When Truman Enos was full of vigor he decided to build his own monument, a veritable ledger of his marital activities. Building the base of small cobblestones, he installed a marble top with eight sides on which he chisled the Enos family history. On one side of the octagonal monument are the words, "Lendy Thrall, 1st wife of Truman Enos, died April 29, 1815, aged 35 years." On another side it reads, "Betsy Campbell, 2nd wife of Truman Enos, died July 2, 1817, aged 26 years." On a third side, the letters showing the lapse of time, is chiseled,

"Abby Parmalee, 3rd wife of Truman Enos, died Jan. 14, 1862, aged 69 years."

Then, as though fashioned by another hand, are the words, "Truman Enos, died May 11, 1869, aged 91 years." The other sides are taken up with records of the death of Lendy Thrall's baby, Talmaget Enos, who was drowned in the Canasawacta shortly after his mother's death. Also space is given to the death of Lendy's brother. One side is still unused. Perhaps it was intended for Clarissa Wood, his last flame. The unusual monument is still drawing the interest of many who visit Mt. Hope cemetery just south of the city line.

Truman Enos died nearly blind and entirely deaf. He died at the home of his daughter in the old Harris homestead, still standing on North Broad Street in Norwich. When his life closed Chenango County lost one of its most picturesque and worthwhile builders.

BRISBEN — CANAL TOWN

Driving through the quiet little hamlet of Brisben, located a few miles south of Oxford in Chenango County, one could hardly believe that this peaceful community, with its new Baptist Church, was once a scene of activity, canal boats, free-for-all fights and plenty of popularity. It was once called Tinkerport because of the canal boat repair shops situated there.

Today Brisben is a friendly residential spot along a busy highway. The postmaster no longer packs brass knuckles and many of the residents no longer lock their doors.

The good people of Brisben go either to the Baptist edifice or a church in Oxford, and there hasn't been a church quarrel there in many years.

The early years of the village were pretty rough and the old timers say that it was the Chenango Canal that gave the village the black eye it carried for many years. The canal ran along beside the town, and there was a tie-up dock directly in the center of the town. Added to that, a large hotel stood nearby and the welcome mat was always out to the canalers to stop for a drink, or to spend the evening among others of their kind. The hostelry even furnished accommodations for the mules that pulled the boats, so that almost every night something was certain to happen in Brisben.

At one time Brisben was called "East Greene" and on some of the older maps it is still so designated. Not only that, but there were two East Greenes, one about two miles south of the other, with an invisible line of demarcation between. To those north of the line the southern neighbors were of little consequence, and vice versa.

When Lorin Miller established the first post office it was below the line, but that was in 1838, when no rivalry existed. Miller also owned a hotel there. Then came Uri King, who still maintained the office on the south side of the line, but when the third postmaster, John Stoughton, was elected he immediately moved the post office north of the line. That may have been the first bone of contention.

151

Then came Postmaster George Race, who moved the post office back to its original place below the line and kept it there for about a year. What pressure was brought to bear is not known, but within the year, Albert Jewell was appointed postmaster and he loaded the post office furniture into a farm wagon and moved it back north of the line, to about its present position. There is no record of its being moved again.

Upper and lower East Greene naturally became antagonistic toward one another for no apparent reason. However the hotel in the lower part of the village burned, and that ended the double village. The hotel and other places of business were never replaced after the fire.

With the abandonment of the canal in 1869, Brisben changed. The rough element that at times had made life a nightmare for the local folks had vanished. Peace reigned, but unfortunately much of the local businesses vanished also.

At one time Brisben had several stores, two hotels, a school, saw mill, a planing and shingle mill, shoe factory, three blacksmith shops, a cheese factory and a lumber mill. The original Baptist church burned and stood where the present church now stands. At the time of the fire, it was considered the oldest Baptist church in the county.

Like many other villages in Chenango County, Brisben has recovered from a lusty past and settled down to become a quiet spot where folks enjoy living. Today, when the church bells ring out on the Sabbath, it is not met with roistering yells and unkind remarks from the canal docks or the hotel porch. No racing livery rigs or runaway horses disturb the calm of the village and no midnight fist fights awaken the peace-loving citizens. Folks like it best this way.

WHEN HOPS WERE KING

If this happened to be the latter part of an August a half century ago, and you were driving through Chenango County at night, you wouldn't wonder at the sound of a dance fiddle coming from behind a big bonfire in a field, or from a barn loft.

Your first words would be, "The hop pickers are having a dance!"

When you got nearer you would see 30 or 40 men, women, boys and girls, prancing around to the calls of the fiddler.

Those were the hop picking days that the oldsters still talk about — days when most farmers raised hops as a cash crop. The hop crop drew men and women from all walks of of life, from all parts of the state, to help with the harvest. Many young people spent two or three weeks of their school vacations picking hops. Doctors, lawyers, businessmen and other professionals even planned their two weeks' vacation so as to coincide with the hop harvest. It was a pleasant time for those who had to live in the cities the rest of the year.

Hops are used in the manufacture of beer, and the hops grown in Central New York were very special hops. The soil of Chenango, Madison, Oneida and adjacent counties seemed best fitted for growing hops. The communities around Waterville were claimed to be the best hop growers.

Back in the hop-growing days, hundreds of acres in Central New York, somewhat resembled Indian villages, with tepee-like arrangements of poles tied together at the top, with four hop vines running up each pole.

It was no easy matter to grow hops. They were not grown from seed, but from pieces of roots from the former growth. These were planted one year and the hops that grew from them were picked the following year.

Many an aging doctor or lawyer of today can look back to the hop picking days — when his education was paid for by his nimble hop-picking fingers. Women were easily the best and fastest pickers, old timers say.

The upright poles were placed in "hills," three or four poles to each hill, and four vines to a pole. Some farmers had a method of using a single pole with strong string tied to the top and fanned out at the bottom, in place of the other three poles. The field of poles had to be cultivated continously to keep the crop growing vigorously.

Picking usually started in mid-August. Four pickers were assigned to a large hop box, capable of holding 28 bushels in four compartments of seven bushels each. Men pickers could pick one of these large boxes a day, while women seemed to be able to fill three or four such boxes. Hops were not easy on the pickers' hands. The sharp petals on the buds often wreaked havoc on the fingers of the picker, many of whom had to wear gloves.

When picked, the hops were placed in kilns, a number of which can still be seen in Central New York. These wooden buildings had a cupola on top to allow the heavy fetid air to pass out, although it was still necessary to leave a small amount of moisture in the hops.

The final job was the baling of the hops. A bale of hops weighed approximately 180 pounds, often more, and these had to be left for the inspection of the prospective buyer, who usually took a generous sample of several pounds at the farmer's expense. If the samples met the approval of his firm, the buyer would sign the purchase order.

When the hops were seasoned over brimstone heat in the kiln and properly aired by the turning of the cupola, they were baled in what was known as hop cloth or hop sacking. A good grade of hops often brought a dollar a pound.

It was fun and hard work and lucrative, but within a few years the drop in the value of hops made it unprofitable to grow them.

THE LAST BLACKSMITH

A little girl stood tearfully before the 82-year-old blacksmith. Unless the man could repair her horse's foot, the animal was doomed. He would have to be shot.

The late A. J. Canny, the last of the old school blacksmiths in Chenango County, agreed to have a look at the horse and went to the home of his young client. The hoof was bad, all right. A member of the family had taken the unshod animal on a pavement, and a large section of the hoof was gone.

"I'll see what I can do with it," the blacksmith said reassuringly in his rich Irish brogue, flashing a grin at the hopeful child. He unwrapped his tools from his leather apron, and in less than an hour the blacksmith had pared part of the remaining hoof and put on a new shoe. Then the other foot was made to conform to it.

"There," the blacksmith said, patting the child on the head, "Your horse is as good as ever. Just go careful for a while and let him get used to his new feet."

When asked the price of his call, the old blacksmith pointed to a place on his cheek.

"See that spot?" he asked. "Well, that little girl threw her arms around my neck and kissed me — an' me with all that dirt and grime from the shop. It was pay enough for any man."

Anthony Canny had the last shop in the Southern Tier and until his passing, he shod horses and pounded out iron work with the strength that would shame a much younger man. The grand old blacksmith of Norwich could fix anything and sparks flew from his anvil from dawn to dusk.

A native of County Clair, Ireland, Canny came to America in 1892. His first job was in a steel mill in Braddock, Pa. In a year he was fed up with the blast furnaces and moved to New York state where he apprenticed himself to a blacksmith, in a shop near what is now the Berglas plant in Norwich. Later he went to a shop on Mechanic St. where he remained 11 years, moving to Fair St. in 1948. Old timers and some not so old timers will recall the jolly old Irishman.

But the village blacksmith is a thing of the past. It really wasn't long ago that the blacksmith shop was one of the most important places in town, especially on rainy days.

In the days when boys did a milking before school, and pulled weeds from a vegetable garden, they were in their glory when father sent them with Old Bess, the bay mare, down to the blacksmith shop on a Saturday morning, to be shod. Boys liked the smell of a blacksmith shop — the smoke that came when fitting the red hot shoe to the horse's hoof, the acrid odor coming from the forge as the shoe got red hot and the sizzling steam ascending to the rafters as the blacksmith tossed the hot shoe into a tub of water.

It was interesting to watch the various horses and how they reacted to the blacksmith. There was that "kicker and biter" of Fuzzy Williams' who was used for general delivery. You couldn't imagine a meaner critter. One couldn't walk past him without the horse making a pass at him with one of his hind feet, or snapping with those yellowing teeth.

But the blacksmith never as much as noticed him, and held the front foot of the critter on his leather apron as he rasped off the surplus hoof material, did the same to his hind feet, without any reaction from the horse, except maybe he would lay his ears back now and then.

Then there was Ellis's old scrawny bay who needed additional treatment. He hated blacksmiths, and this necessitated the use of a "Twist", an instrument that made a nasty horse think twice. It consisted of a leather thong that was placed over the upper lip of the horse and gently twisted by the owner or helper. It didn't take many twists to make the horse decide that discretion was the better part of valor. As the shoeing went on the twist could be loosened until the horse forgot all about being ornery, until the next time.

The blacksmith was the mechanic of the town. What he could not make with iron just could not be made. In those days gone by, there were always some old codgers who arrived at the shop early and stayed until the owner banked the fire in his forge for the night. These old fellows often served as "fly switchers" and kept the flies away from the more skittish horses. For this purpose a real horse's tail was fastened to a broom handle and could be swung over the animal's back, keeping flies away from the horse and the busy blacksmith working on him.

Many questions of public moment were discussed in the blacksmith shop. There were always answers to questions of state. The elections of presidents, governors and even dog catchers were decided in advance by the sitters who occupied soap boxes, nail kegs and even chairs some had brought from home.

Crack shots told of their prowess and many fish were caught and lost around the sawdust box that served as a spittoon. The smell of soft coal and "long-cut" smoking tobacco was ever present and joined with the other natural odors of the shop, making it something never to be forgotten.

The old blacksmith shops are gone. In their places stand unromantic garages and gasoline stations. The old nail keg congress is also gone and the affairs of the nation must be decided by other minds. But to those who remember, the clang of the blacksmith's hammer against the anvil, and the heavy feet of the farm horses on the plank floor, will ever be fresh in memory.

THE VANISHED BREED

An old rusted-out coffee pot, a few corroded tin cans, gunny sacks that fall apart when one touches them and the remains of tarpaper which had been used for a lean-to were all that was left of another era, when I first came to Norwich and wanted to do a story about the knights of the road.

The locale was near the DL&W railroad tracks, just south of the city, by a bridge that spanned the Canasawacta Creek. It was just outside the city limits, behind what is now a shopping center on Rt. 12.

It was reminiscent of the era of the train-riding hobo, at one time the bane of the railroads and small town police. He was a general nuisance to farmers and householders.

There was not a farmhouse where the wandering tramp did not call. He even invaded the cities, calling at the back doors of homes asking for a handout. It is said that if the lady of the house gave him a good meal, he would mark the place so that his friends might also stop there and enjoy the same good fortune. A certain mark on the sidewalk in front of the house, or a nick in the bark of a tree that stood by the front of the home, meant the occupants were generous and good cooks!

To arrest a hobo got a constable nowhere. He had committed no crime according to the laws of his day, and to be put in jail overnight was just what he wanted. It meant a "meal of vittles" and a bunk for the night, even if it was on newspapers on the cold floor. In the morning he would be given a breakfast and sent on his way.

No one has been able to fathom the depth of a hobo's thinking. Why would he rather starve himself, sleep in a barn or under a haystack, than to do a stroke of work and live like other folks? Why did he steer away from the bathtub, the razor and the chance to wear clean clothes? Why did he prefer to wear the ill-fitting things which he had been given or which he had snatched from a clothesline?

"I have seen as many as 30 tramps sleeping on the floor or on top of the cells in our Norwich station house" former Police Chief Mattice told me. "Now it is over. We used to give them coffee in the morning and send them on their way."

It is now against the rules for a police station to give lodging or food to anyone unless there is a charge against him. This may have had something to do with the falling off of the hobo business in small towns, although the advent of the truck and the vigilance of the police have gone far toward keeping such men away from the wandering fever.

The late Herbert Davis, for many years a Norwich policeman, told me some years ago that it was a regular Sunday afternoon job to "clean out the jungle" that lay near the tracks south of the city. There were seldom any arrests, but if the cleanup could be made an hour before the afternoon freight came along there would be a chance of success.

"They were usually harmless fellows," Davis said. "But folks were afraid for their chickens and the bacon in their smokehouses. So we had to clean 'em out regularly."

It was seldom that one of the tramp fraternity would work unless driven to it by hunger. He chose to take his chances at someone's door, and it was surprising how successful he was.

The successful tramp always had a good story to tell the sympathetic housewife, and the better the story the better the food. His misfortune was never his own fault. From long experience he knew exactly how to tell it. He tried to make his call when the husband was away. Husbands usually were too wise to fall for a concocted story. Or perhaps they resented the freedom the hobo represented.

Generally the tramp fared pretty well. At least he had a variety of food and lodging places. He saw much of the country. He knew where every "jungle" was located and who he might see there. If he was a wanderer who remained in one part of the state, he knew most of the police officers, he was often friendly with them and was never too bashful to ask favors.

Sometimes if it was a nice day and several "bo's" happened to meet at the jungle at the same time, they would each take a section of the city and only ask for a turnip or a few potatoes, an onion or carrots. They met back at the jungle at a given time, and all the pilfered vegetables ended up in a rusty can, over a campfire. Most all homes had a little garden out back so it was not much effort to find the proper ingedients. Without a doubt some unusual stew recipes passed on with the hobo.

Once in a while a lady would lose a pie she had set on the window sill to cool, but this was the "piece de resistance."

It has been nearly 40 years since the Norwich hobo jungle existed. Two decades have passed since the boys at the station house, coming on duty at 7 in the morning had to open all the windows and air out the left over fragrance of the open road travelers. It had been a long time since the 1930's when hoboing was at its best in Chenango County.

While police and householders may miss the familiar character, he marked an era of freedom and generosity that may never return.

Unlike the canal rowdies, the hobo seldom drank or fought. Perhaps it was the fact that he had no money to spend so foolishly, or perhaps the country had progressed enough to form a new breed.

Whatever the reason, we shed no tears over his absence.

ROY GALLINGER

The late Roy Gallinger was born on a hilltop farm in lower Canada and learned his ABCs in a tiny red schoolhouse on the outskirts of Kingston, Ontario. His father, a bricklayer by trade, brought his family of six boys and a girl to the United States where he would have more opportunities for work, and settled with his family in Cayuga County, where his sons and daughter grew up.

Roy became a writer, first as a columnist on a rural newspaper, and later was the editor and publisher of the *Marcellus Observer*, in Onondaga County. Early in his newspaper career he established his "Roving with Roy" column, telling of incidents which took place among his readers along the country roads. At the same time he wrote a weekly "Scotts Mills" bit, a humorous column telling of the doings in the imaginary village of Scotts Mills. This column was later syndicated.

He was well known for his twice-weekly radio script, "Letter to the Editor," which was broadcast over radio station WCHN. Until his retirement in 1970, he was a member of the editorial staff of the Syracuse *Herald-American*, and of the Syracuse *Post Standard*. His column "Around Chenango County" which appeared in the Syracuse *Herald-Journal* received wide acceptance in the area.